HELP!

I'M LOCKED UP...
AND I NEED HOPE!

HELP!

I'M LOCKED UP...
AND I NEED HOPE!

BY

LYNN POTTER

Published by Lynn Potter

ISBN-10: 1-4664087-3-1
ISBN-13: 978-1-4664-0873-9

Cover and Interior Design by Three Monkey Media - threemonkeymedia.com
Cover Image by Fuse/Jupiterimages

Dedication

I dedicate this book to all the beautiful women and young ladies that I have had the opportunity to meet and spend time with who have passed through the doors of Moss Justice Center in York, S.C. over the years.

Without these precious women, I would not have had the inspiration to complete this work. Their stories, love, questions and challenges have made me a stronger, more compassionate person than any amount of theological training could have taught me.

I have been known to tell family and friends that if anyone is serious about seminary, they need to spend time in their local jail or prison. The ministry education learned there could never come from a textbook.

We have laughed, cried, danced, sang, and shared scripture. We have questioned, challenged, and stretched each other's beliefs. In the midst of seemingly utter chaos, the Spirit of God swells in the blocks and we are struck silent. It is very much like the book of Genesis where we read that God's Spirit hovered over the chaos and spoke light into the darkness.

We have experienced Divine intervention and without any prodding ladies embrace each other and forgive as I sit by awestruck. We speak into each other's lives with comfort and hope. We try to coach each other into being honest with ourselves, each other, and God.

I have had more "Church" inside the confines of Moss Justice than in many meetings I attend on a regular basis. I believe there is something about having the freedom to realize that we are all a mess and need help that allows God's Spirit to move among us. We come together knowing that we need Him to intervene in our lives and learn together just how powerfully wonderful He is.

I leave Moss Justice every visit with the sense of God's presence among us. I leave a better person every time.

Thank you, women and young ladies of Moss Justice for some of the best times in my life. I look forward to meeting you all when the trumpet blows and we are gathered together in the sky with Him.

Remember, none of you will be wearing orange issued clothing! No more wrist bands with numbers identifying you; you will be wearing a white wedding gown and a glowing gold wedding band. Our King and Bridegroom will have come to rescue us.

We will meet at the wedding supper of the Lamb! (Revelation 19:6-9)

Until then, I dedicate this book to you and your willingness to share your lives with me.

All my love,

Ms. Lynn

Contents

Introduction

This workbook is a study of the first two chapters of the book of Hosea in the Old Testament. It is an invitation for you to grasp hold of hope in the midst of your crisis. It is an invitation to see the rainbow in the midst of the rain. It is an invitation for you to see God's hand in your life when you can't see His face. It is an invitation for you to hope against hope.

Through the following pages we will examine some of the principles in the book of Hosea and see how they relate to our lives. There are exercises in the course of our journey that invite you to get real with yourself and God. Some of them may be difficult. Some may not. In either case, I encourage you to take your time with each one.

There is no right or wrong answer. There is no one who will be grading you. There is only freedom at the end if you will open yourself up to the truth. The Bible says that we will know the truth, and the truth will set us free. (John 8:32) This is what I am offering you through this study.

You are not alone in the journey. The Spirit of Truth is your guide. (John 16:13) As I have written this book, I too, have reflected on the exercises as they relate to my life. May you find hope in these pages that you are in the will of God and that He wants to comfort you right where you are.

I have written this book for those who are behind bars, or *locked up*, as we say. Although these precious ones are the ones I have specifically written to, I believe the principles in this book may be used by those of us who are physically free but *locked up* emotionally. Whatever state you find yourself in, Hosea is an incredible story of hope and love. No matter how many times we fail, we can rely on the God of Hosea to woo us back to Himself while He disciplines us.

God bless you as you begin your journey to the truth; the truth that will set you free.

CHAPTER 1
"Embracing Restraint"

"Trust in the lord with all your heart,
And lean not on your own understanding;
In all your ways acknowledge Him,
And He shall direct your paths."
Proverbs 3:5, 6

Before we begin, I would like to share a short story with you from my life. Those of you who know me personally from Moss Justice might get a kick out of this if you remember some of our worship times. Those of you who don't, well I trust you will learn something here.

I am the kind of person who tends to go all the way with something if I enjoy it or believe in it. Many times that wasn't the best thing to do but we will leave that for another time. What I want to share with you today is an experience I had during worship in church one Sunday.

I am a person who loves to dance, shout, run around, wave banners, and stomp my feet. Keeping this in mind as you read, you will understand what restraint feels like to me. It will also preface the intention of this book; that restraint can be a good thing. Let me share with you what I wrote in my journal the following day after I felt the restraining hand of God:

I sat on the seat thinking, "This is what it's like for someone in a wheelchair." I felt the restraint, the hopelessness, and the defeat as I looked at my legs. I wanted to run and jump and dance. I rubbed my hands up and down my legs feeling the roughness of my blue jeans. I rubbed my belly where the scar was from a recent surgery. I was antsy and longing; longing with everything in me. "Please let me out!" I cried inside. I wanted to shout, "Those of you who can move, MOVE! Don't miss your opportunity. Don't waste a minute of this freedom you have. Get up and DO SOMETHING!"

The room was full of excitement. The band was jamming and filling the air with all my favorite songs. This is what I wait for. "It's in my bones," they say. Every fiber of my being comes alive in this atmosphere. I dare to walk where angels walk, to see what angels see, to hear what angels hear. I dare to sing with them and the great cloud of witnesses who say;

> "You are worthy to take the scroll,
> And to open its seals; for you were slain,
> And have redeemed us to God by Your blood
> Out of every tribe and tongue and people and nation,
> And have made us kings and priests to our God;
> And we shall reign on the earth." (Revelation 5:9- 10)

And, I dare to dance with King Jesus. But today my dancing was over and I don't mind telling you I felt defeated, ripped off, and cranky!

"I recognized that it was God standing beside me, protecting me, caring for me, and loving me through this humble man."

"That's all the dancing for you today," a man leaned close enough for me to hear. He had come from the other side of the room to speak to me. I nodded, knowing he was right. The music played on, teasing me, taunting me, calling me. I sat down and the man stood in the row behind me. There was something powerful about his presence.

I felt as though I was sitting at the foot of a huge mountain. It towered over me yet there was comfort in its size. I remember hearing a still small voice. It said, *"He's got your back."* I felt very safe and I smiled. I recognized that it was God standing behind me, protecting me, caring for me, and loving me through this humble man.

Later, I thought about what had happened. This man saw something. He cared and He came to me. What did he see? I suspect it was something God had shown him; something I couldn't see at the time.

I remembered the man speaking to me earlier that morning. He said "I will dance for you today." Why did he say that? I laughed when I thought about my reply, "You'll have to step up the pace if you're going to dance in *my* place."

Later, during worship, I knelt on the floor and began to sway. Again, this man came to me. He helped me to my feet. He guided me back to my seat and said, "Come sit. I'm concerned about you." No longer was this man just a gentle man, but a vessel of the living God who wanted to speak to me, His child.

I still could not understand the restriction God had placed on me. I thought I was ready to cut loose just a bit. I knew in my heart the man was right and that God had sent him to me, but I found myself pouting. I kept rubbing my legs thinking, *this is just not fair!* I thought for SURE I was ready. But, apparently, God didn't.

At that point, I had a choice to make. I could sit there miserable, feeling defeated, ripped off and cranky, or I could make the best of a bad situation and worship where I was.

> **"*I could sit there miserable, feeling defeated, ripped off and cranky, or I could make the best of a bad situation and worship where I was.*"**

I was feeling the restriction, the restraining hand of God on my life.

Restraint tends to carry with it negative feelings. We hear things like, "She's out of control, come help me restrain her." Or, "I've got to get a restraining order on him; he's liable to kill someone." We could be restrained by shackles, hand cuffs, tether straps, or any number of things. Restraint by its very definition is *taking away control.* It means to limit, to restrict, or stop someone from doing something.

This is what happened to me in the short story I just shared. I wanted to do something that I was not ready for. Who knows what harm this brother saved me from? Who knows what God knew?

In my thinking, I knew the doctor was releasing me to go back to work the following week *without restriction.* I was feeling pretty spunky when I got there and thought I'd be ok if I didn't exert too much energy. I did, of course, tone it down a bit. I did not run up and down the aisles, I walked. I did not move quickly but swayed. I did not twirl like I normally do, but turned slowly.

Even so, God had ordained a restriction on my body to give it the rest and time it needed to heal. He gave the doctor wisdom to decide how long that time would be. *I stepped out of those boundaries and felt the gentle restraining hand of God.*

In my case, I was literally put in my place. I had to sit still while everyone who wanted to was free to move around. I had to sit there and watch the flags waving, the pastor dancing while playing his guitar, and the people moving all to my favorite music. I felt like I was in a straight jacket.

At first, I cried out to God questioning what was going on. "Surely, God, You don't mean for me to sit here and do nothing? Don't You realize how HARD this is for me? How much longer will I have to stay here like this? I was envious and felt useless. *I felt like a caged animal.* Does any of this sound familiar? Have you had any of these feelings lately?

> **"***As I started to understand the benefits of the restraint that was put on me, I was changed. I was able to sit there and just be loved by God.***"**

Restraint is not fun but sometimes restraint is necessary. The longer I sat there, the more confined I felt. But you know what changed it for me? I began to worship with what I had. I could not run, dance, twirl, or wave a banner with my body but I could do it with my heart. As I began to worship quietly from my heart, God started showing me some extraordinary things. He showed me His love for me. He showed me the protection He provides for me. He showed me He cares for me and cares about what happens to me. He showed me He surrounds me with His love even when I am feeling frustrated.

As I started to understand the benefits of the restraint that was put on me, I was changed. I was able to sit there and just be loved by God.

I trust as we take this journey together the same thing will happen for you. I trust that God will show you His unlimited, perfect love. I trust that you, like me, will be set free as you *embrace your restraint.*

What does *your present restraint* feel like? What do you want to accomplish by proceeding with this study? Write your thoughts here:

_____

_____

_____

_____

_____

_____

_____

_____

_____

CHAPTER 2
"Don't Give Up"

"Now hope does not disappoint,
because the love of God
has been poured out in our hearts
by the Holy Spirit
who was given to us."
Romans 5:5

As we proceed on our journey, let's take an inventory of what our beliefs are concerning God. We all have our individual thoughts and reasons for them. In this short chapter, I would like to give you an opportunity to examine your thinking and write down where you are in your relationship with God.

This is very important because how we view God determines how we live our lives. Is He a distant, unattainable being? Is He a big Santa Clause in the sky we only come to with our wish lists once a year? Is He a mean Father that only punishes or abuses us? Is He an angry judge waiting to slam His gavel down on the bench? Do you feel God is someone you can trust to do the right thing all the time? Is He someone you can count on to be there for you? Or, is He someone you don't believe in at all?

Most of us have a very twisted view of God because of the things that have happened in our lives. We tend to view God through the eyes of our circumstances. For instance, through the years, my relationship with my father deteriorated until it was non-existent. This clouded my image of God as my Father. I had a very hard time relating to a loving, caring God who would never leave me like the Bible says. I had to agree with the Bible, but I did not have that assurance in my heart. It has taken many years of God healing my heart to experience that truth.

I am in no way blaming my father, just relating to you how I came to have a distorted picture of God. We are not here to play the blame game, but just to do a reality check to see how we view God.

Take a minute to think through how *you* view God. Jot down some thoughts that come to mind. Take your time. Be honest with yourself.

_____
_____
_____
_____
_____

Do you believe you have a twisted view of God? Why or why not?
Who might have contributed to this twisted view and why? _____
_____
_____
_____
_____
_____

I want to share with you a simple but enlightening statement that Paul makes in Romans. I like how the Life Recovery Bible puts it:

"Notice how God is both kind and severe. He is severe to those who disobeyed, but kind to you if you continue to trust in his kindness. But if you stop trusting, you also will be cut off." (Romans 11:22)

> **"We either look at God shaking in fear because of things we have done, or we ignore Him thinking His love will never discipline us.."**

Here we see two distinct sides of God's character. They are His kindness and His discipline. At times we gravitate too far to one side or the other. We either look at God shaking in fear because of things we have done, or we ignore Him thinking His love will never discipline us. What we need to do is embrace God in His entirety, both His goodness and His discipline.

That is what we are going to do as we read, study, and apply the principles of Hosea to our lives. We are going to learn much about ourselves and God as we take the journey through this book. We are going to learn to open our hearts up to ourselves, to God, and see our situation from His point of view.

We are going to be challenged to get real, get honest, and in the end be set free from the damaging things that have controlled us for so long. We are going to see that in the *midst of our crisis,* God is loving and compassionate. We will come to believe that He has allowed us to be where we are *because of His love.*

I invite you to continue with this in mind; *God is for you, He is not against you.* Whatever twists and turns your life has taken, He is not surprised. He has not forgotten you, *nor is He out to get you.* His only desire is that you will come to Him as your only hope and that you will realize that His discipline is His love for you.

We read in Hebrews 12:5-8 from the Life Recovery Bible:

> "**I invite you to continue with this in mind; God is for you, He is not against you.**"

> "And have you forgotten the encouraging words God spoke to you as his children? He said, 'My child, don't make light of the LORD's discipline, and don't give up when he corrects you. For the LORD disciplines those he loves, and he punishes each one he accepts as his child.' As you endure this divine discipline, remember that God is treating you as his own children. Whoever heard of a child who is never disciplined by its father? If God doesn't discipline you as he does all of His children, it means that you are illegitimate and are not really his children at all."

What are your thoughts on the above verses? How do they apply in your current situation? Take some time to meditate on the verses and write out your thoughts.

_____
_____
_____
_____
_____
_____
_____
_____
_____
_____
_____
_____
_____
_____
_____

Do you believe God loves you right where you are? Why or why not?

_____

_____

_____

_____

_____

_____

_____

Before we move on, I would like to give you an opportunity to talk to God about what you have just written. He knows how you feel already so feel free to be honest with Him. You might want to write out a prayer to Him or just take some time to meditate...

_____

_____

_____

_____

_____

_____

_____

Do you feel you are you ready to continue to experience both the kindness and the discipline of the Lord in your life? Are you ready to receive hope in the midst of your crisis?

Will you say...

"No matter what it looks like, I am not going to give up. I am going to receive hope right where I am. I am going to trust that God loves me; He is for me, and not against me. I am going to believe that His discipline is His love for me because I am His beloved child."

If so, come, follow me...

CHAPTER 3
"Support System Inventory"

…If God is for us
Who can be against us…?
Romans 8:31

Hosea is one of my favorite books in the Bible. It brings me hope every time I read it. It is a tender story of God's love and His desire to deliver His children from bondage.

I would encourage you (if you have a Bible available,) to read the first two chapters of the book of Hosea in the Old Testament to get an idea of what we will be studying and talking about. Ask God to open your eyes as you read. You may want to get some extra writing paper in case you want to write more than this book has given space for. You may want to go over this study more than once. I encourage you to re-read what you have written during this study from time to time.

I find that notes I have written help me years down the road as most of my problems reoccur in different situations and it is very helpful to re-read my thoughts. They remind me of God's love and care during a trial I might be going through.

I want to pray for you before we continue:

Lord, I ask that you be with Your daughter right now as she reads this material and does the lessons in this book. I pray that Your Spirit would guide and direct all thoughts and emotions and that great healing and deliverance would transpire. I pray that Your name would be lifted up above all names and that You would be pleased with what is accomplished through these lessons. May Your daughter be encouraged to fight the good fight of faith and come out on the other side of this crisis better for it. In Jesus' mighty name I pray. Amen.

We shall begin this session by reading Hosea 2:14- 15:

> "Therefore, behold, I will allure her, Will bring her into the wilderness, and speak comfort to her. I will give her her vinyards from there and the Valley of Achor as a door of hope. She shall sing there, As in the days of her youth, As in the day when she came up from the land of Egypt."

As I re-read this passage, I am struck by something. It seems to me that God does things much differently than I would. I'm thinking; *Send me to the wilderness to speak comfort to me and give me stuff from there? That doesn't even make sense. Why would You do that?*

The Bible tells us God's ways are better than our ways.

Read with me Isaiah 55:8-9:

> "For My thoughts are not your thoughts, nor are your ways My ways, says the Lord. For as the heavens are higher than the earth, so are My ways higher than your ways and my thoughts than your thoughts."

The implication here is that *we don't see the whole picture, but God does.* That can be a bit frustrating, especially when we find ourselves locked up. We are at the mercy of those who have been given authority over us and the simplest of decisions have been taken away from us. No longer can we choose when to rise or go to bed. When we shower, brush our teeth, and meal times are now subject to the institution's time schedule. We are searched, our dignity invaded at any given time, and our privacy becomes non-existent. At any time a line of officers may come into our space and require us to stand at attention at the end of our beds as they rummage through our meager possessions. We then may be required to call out our "number" for roll call. If we are not careful, we can become just a number to ourselves as well.

> **"***I want to help you understand that you have not been forgotten completely, no matter what has happened in your life with your family and friends.* **"**

There is good news, however. You may be thinking, *what could that possibly be?* I want to show you something through this passage in Hosea that might give you some hope as you find yourself a ward of the state. I want to help you understand that you have not been forgotten completely, no matter what has happened in your life with your family and friends.

Many times as we make the downward spiral that lands us in jail or prison, we have burned many bridges. We find that we have caused family members and friends much pain and sorrow. Or, we find that we have had been hanging out with the wrong people. We thought they were our friends but realize they are of no comfort in our present predicament. We may have essentially lost every meaningful relationship we have ever had.

No matter how you fall on the scale of one to ten as far as relationships go, I want to encourage you that *all is not lost*. If I were to ask you to name the relationships that are meaningful to you right now, would you have the courage to stick with me while we analyze what's going on with them?

I am going to give you some space here to list those who you care about and on a scale of one to ten, one being destroyed and ten being healthy, rate those relationships before you got locked up and how you see them now. If you need more space, feel free to use an extra piece of paper.

(Remember, every exercise we do in this book needs to be done with as much honesty as possible.) Many of our lives have been spent getting what we want or what we think we need by manipulation, half-truths, or downright lies. Owning up to this is the first step to freedom.

The Bible says the truth will set us free. It would be good for you to look that up and read it a couple of times, even write it out before you begin.

It is found in John 8:32 in the New Testament. If you do not have a Bible, here is what is says:

> "And you shall know the truth and the truth shall make you free."

Write John 8:32 out here before we begin. In your own words, ask God to help you look at these relationships truthfully.

_____

_____

_____

_____

_____

In the spaces below rate your relationships:

Person	Before being locked up (1-10)	After being locked up (1-10)
_____	_____	_____
_____	_____	_____
_____	_____	_____
_____	_____	_____
_____	_____	_____
_____	_____	_____

Now, I would encourage you to take some time and think about why you gave each relationship the score you did. If you realize some have been destroyed due to your part in its demise, find the courage to look deep into the situation and see if there is anything, small as it may seem, that you could do right now to set things right.

If you see that some of the relationships you had prior to being locked up are not good for you, perhaps you need to take a good look at what drew you into the relationship in the first place. Then ask God to help you sever it in the right way.

What we are doing here is taking an inventory of your support system. I want to help you see where you are in terms of support. These relationships may be either on the outside or the inside. They are healthy or toxic, good or bad.

Has the relationship produced positive or negative things? Has the relationship built you up or torn you down? Has it caused you to do the right thing or the wrong thing?

"Be honest with yourself. Although the truth may cause you pain, in the end it will set you free."

Here's where complete honesty is necessary. We can look at situations with clouded vision because we want to believe the best of people, or we are strapped by circumstances to certain people. Don't let clouded vision rob you of the freedom you can receive by being honest. For instance, if your child's daddy is an abuser, don't make excuses for him; give the relationship the low score it deserves. Be honest with yourself. Although the truth may cause you pain, in the end it will set you free.

Give each relationship the time it deserves to search your heart for the truth. Pray as you are doing this exercise that you will see the truth. This is a lifetime exercise. Be mindful of the people you associate with and what the relationships produce in your life. Look for the good in people but don't be blinded by circumstances when a relationship needs to be severed.

This goes for all your relationships, both inside and out.

May God bless you as you take this step of faith and courage to seek the truth about how those around you have affected your life!

Person	Relationship rate (1-10)	Reason
	1 completely destructive - 10 completely healthy	
_____	_____	_____
_____	_____	_____
_____	_____	_____
_____	_____	_____
_____	_____	_____
_____	_____	_____

In the next lesson, we will examine our relationship with God and how that fits into what we read from Hosea at the beginning of this chapter.

I know you will be excited to see what God can do with your situation as we move from the natural relationships in our lives to the spiritual relationship we have with God.

I want to encourage you to pray continually that you will be able to understand God's desire to develop a permanent healthy relationship with you that will last your lifetime no matter where you are.

A new life is waiting for you if you will heed the words of Jesus, *You will know the truth and the truth will set you free.* (John 8:32)

Let's move on and search for that truth together...

CHAPTER 4
"Come to Me"

"Come to Me,
all you who labor and are heavy laden
and I will give you rest."
Matthew 11:28

"No power in the sky above
Or in the earth below—
Indeed, nothing in all creation
Will ever be able to separate us
From the love of God
That is revealed in Christ Jesus our Lord."
Romans 8:39
(Life Recovery Bible)

In the last exercise, we looked into relationships that we have had throughout our lives and attempted to see the truth concerning them. I hope you have taken this seriously and spent enough time to see each one for what it really is.

As we journey along together, I want to give you the opportunity to examine your life and your heart to see where you stand with God. I encourage you to take off the masks; the ones that you have worn for so long and stare yourself in the face. If you aren't willing to do that, none of what we are trying to accomplish here will mean a hill of beans. In other words, it just won't work.

If you are ready to get real, let's move on. After being truthful with yourself about the relationships in your life, I want to challenge you to examine the most important relationship you will ever have. This is the relationship you have with God. As with the other relationships, I am asking you to rate it from one to ten. (One being non-existent and ten being an ongoing, minute by minute, close relationship.) Along with the score, I am going to ask you to write down why you have given it that particular score and then invite you to write a letter to God explaining why you feel as you do.

In the meantime, read Matthew 9:4. It tells us Jesus knows what we are thinking. So, don't try to hide anything when you are writing. God knows our every thought even before we think it. He knows all about us and *loves us anyway*. This letter is to set you free to get to know yourself better and draw closer to God. Even if you give yourself a one on the scale, just by writing the letter, you will be moving from a one to a two!

My relationship to God on a scale from one to ten is _____
(Remember 1= non-existent up to 10= minute by minute close relationship)

The reason I gave my relationship to God a score of _____ is because:

_____
_____
_____

Dear God, _____

_____
_____
_____
_____
_____

I want to pause here for a moment to give you a chance to come to God through His Son Jesus if you haven't already. Perhaps you have known God through Jesus but have not been living the life Jesus died to give you. Maybe you have gone down the wrong path and just need the opportunity to regroup, repent, and rededicate your life to God. If you fall into any one of these categories, please continue to read and come home to God for good!

Jesus said in John 14:6 that He is the way, the truth, and the life. He states that no one can come to the Father (God) but by Him. In John 6:44, Jesus says that no one can come to Him (Jesus) unless the Father (God) draws him. John 16:13 says The Spirit of Truth (The Holy Spirit) will guide us into all truth.

As we read the above verses, we see that there is a partnership between God, Jesus, and The Holy Spirit that brings us home to God.

God is not slack concerning His promise but is patient with us. The Bible says He does not want anyone to perish but wants everyone to come to repentance. (2Peter 3:9) That's me, and that's you! He does NOT want you to perish, but come to repentance and come home to Him.

> *"I KNOW God is calling you to Himself and you can stop everything right now and come to Him. JUST AS YOU ARE."*

Today is the day of salvation! If you have stayed with me this long, I KNOW God is calling you to Himself and you can stop everything right now and come to Him. JUST AS YOU ARE.

DON'T DELAY any longer. Don't wrestle with your mind. Come to Him. He is calling you. He loves you *just as you are*. You don't have to "clean up" your act. He will help you. Just come. Come. Right now. Come.

I am going to write out a prayer that you may want to use. If you want to, you can write your own prayer to God. Either way, run into God's waiting arms where you will be received with love and eternal life.

Dear God,
I know I've made a mess of things. I can't seem to get my life together and I know that without You I am totally lost. I believe You sent Your Son Jesus to die on my behalf for my sins. I believe in my heart that You raised Him from the dead and that He is the only way back to You. Please forgive my sins. I ask Jesus to come into my life to live in me, to guide me, and to help me live my life pleasing to You. Thank You for hearing my prayer and bringing me into Your family. Help me from this moment on to live for You. In Jesus' name, Amen.

If you have prayed that prayer or written one similar, be assured that Jesus heard you and has come to live in you and help you. Heaven rejoices when one sinner comes home, and that's YOU!

Let's move on and begin the journey of learning to live lives that Jesus died to give us. Remember, *God is on our side!* No matter what, *God is on our side.*

Read Romans 8: 31-39 from the Life Recovery Bible before we continue. Keep this passage in the back of your mind at all times as we work through this study:

> "What shall we say about such wonderful things as these? If God is for us, who can ever be against us? Since he did not spare even his own Son but gave him up for us all, won't he also give us everything else? Who dares accuse us whom God has chosen for his own? No one—for God himself has given us right standing with himself. Who

then will condemn us? No one—for Christ Jesus died for us and was raised to life for us, and he is sitting in the place of honor at God's right hand, pleading for us. Can anything ever separate us from Christ's love? Does it mean he no longer loves us if we have trouble or calamity, or are persecuted, or hungry, or destitute, or in danger, or threatened with death? (As the scriptures say, "For your sake we are killed every day; we are being slaughtered like sheep.") No, despite all these things, overwhelming victory is ours through Christ, who loved us. And I am convinced that nothing can ever separate us from God's love. Neither death nor life, neither angels nor demons, neither our fears for today nor our worries about tomorrow—not even the powers of hell can separate us from God's love. No power in the sky above or in the earth below—indeed, nothing in all creation will ever be able to separate us from the love of God that is revealed in Christ Jesus our lord."

Say it with me before we continue:

Nothing can separate me from God's love, not jail, not prison, not addiction, not sorrow, not failure, not guilt, not...

You make your own list!

_____
_____
_____
_____
_____
_____
_____
_____
_____
_____
_____

THANK YOU GOD THAT NOTHING CAN SEPARATE US FROM YOUR LOVE!

CHAPTER 5
"Evicting False Gods"

"I am the Lord Your God...,
...You shall have no other gods before me."
Exodus 20:2-3

When we find ourselves locked up, perhaps without friends or family support, we tend to feel like we have been stuck in a desert without water and all we can see for miles in any direction is sand. We see no help. We see no future. We find ourselves existing without hope.

We've completed some exercises to examine our relationships and get a better perspective on where we stand with them. I'm sure while you are locked up, no matter how supportive people are on the outside, there are times that you feel utterly alone. It happens to the best of us. Those of us who feel we have no support system or a destructive one may feel even more alone.

This is where I ask you to stick with me and give faith a chance. I believe if we read Hosea together, we can find some purpose to the madness that is trying to strangle you right now. I believe you can come away from this study thinking differently. I believe you can come away thankful that you are loved as much as you are. Again, I ask you to *give faith a chance*.

Let's read our passage again so that we can recall what we are studying.

Hosea 2:14-15
> "Therefore, behold, I will allure her, Will bring her into the wilderness, and speak comfort to her. I will give her her vineyards from there And the Valley of Achor as a door of hope. She shall sing there, As in the days of her youth. As in the day when she came up from the land of Egypt."

What we need to realize in this paragraph is who we are reading about. It appears that we have two characters in the narrative. If I were to suggest to you that one of the characters is God and the other is you how would you feel about that?

As with anything we read in the Bible, we must look to the things that are said ahead of what we are reading. (Especially if our text starts with words like, *therefore*.) Therefore what? Therefore is a word that is used as a bridge. It tells us that the words prior to this statement are directly involved with what is going on and we need to know the whole story behind what we are reading.

So, before we dive into Hosea 2:14-15 to see how it relates to our lives, and in particular, our incarcerated lives, we need to go back to the beginning of the book of Hosea and see what was going on.

I trust that after we are finished with this study, you will be encouraged and hopeful no matter what is going on in your life. I promise you will see things differently and find a way to *harness hope in the midst of your crisis*. I will show you how you can take this story in Hosea and see how it relates to your situation.

You will learn how to read these passages, see yourself in them, and experience hope as you watch God bring His children back into relationship with Him. You will come to realize that the people who are written about in the Bible are people just like us. They have experienced the same hurts and hang ups, and have made some of the same poor choices we have.

Isn't it comforting to know that when we really mess up, God shows us in the Bible that we are no different than any of His other children? We can find comfort in their stories because we will see that God is patient over and over again with them no matter how far away they drift away from Him.

> **"***Isn't it comforting to know that when we really mess up, God shows us in the Bible that we are no different than any of His other children?* **"**

I encourage you to pray right now and thank God that He has never walked away from you and has stayed by your side even when you were not doing the right thing or even acknowledging Him in your life. Thank Him that He has brought you to the place where you are willing to trust Him with your life.

Ask Him to help you understand your life, your relationship to Him, and what He is doing with you as you read and learn from our study together.

You may want to write out your prayer and read it sometime later to remind you of what you have prayed:

_____

_____

_____

_____

_____

Hosea was a prophet. A prophet in the Old Testament was one who was chosen by God to speak God's words to the people. These words could be of encouragement, warnings, or instruction.

To understand Hosea a little bit better, let's begin with his name. In Bible times, names were very important. Parents named their children to speak into their lives and sow seed into their character. Hosea comes from a root word in the Hebrew language which means "salvation, or deliverance." From this we can see that Hosea's destiny was to be a prophet who would pronounce God's word to His people and His intentions to save them and deliver them.

In 2 Timothy 3:16-17 we read:

> "All scripture is given by inspiration of God, and is profitable for doctrine, for reproof, for correction, for instruction in righteousness, that the man of God may be complete, thoroughly equipped for every good work."

By this we understand that as we read the story in Hosea, we can be instructed in the way to live our lives by the examples that are given to us. We can take what is happening to the people in the story and look at our own lives to see where we have fallen into the same traps they have. We can also see what we can do to get out of those traps and live our lives the way God intended us to. We will also find that He is there every step of the way even when it doesn't seem like it.

To me, it's fascinating to see how similar my life story is to those that I am reading about. I trust you will say the same thing by the time we are finished with this study.

Now, back to Hosea. Let us begin in the first chapter and read a couple of verses there and comment on them. Remember, Hosea was a prophet and he was called to show the people something. In this case, his life was going to be the message.

We can relate to this by thinking of how an officer might bring us a message. Perhaps he wants to show us what happens when contraband is found in someone's possession during a shake down. The offender might be placed in front of everyone and the officer may explain what is likely to happen. In this case, the inmate's situation is the object lesson, thus we have received the intended message.

As we read Hosea chapter one, keep this in mind. Hosea's life was to be the example, the message from God. God was trying to show His people how He felt when they walked away from Him and pursued other gods. To Him, it felt like a wife cheating on her husband. He had given them everything and still they looked to other gods to satisfy their desires.

Hosea did as God asked and married Gomer. Gomer was a woman who could not keep herself within the boundaries of their marriage. She was unfaithful to him. As Hosea experienced this pain in his life, he was able to relate to how God felt when His people went after other gods and walked away from Him. Therefore, Hosea had life experience to back up his words to the people.

In verse 2 of Hosea chapter 1, we read:

> "...For the land has committed great harlotry,
>   by departing from the Lord."

What does it mean to depart from the Lord? During this time in history, the people of God were moving away from righteous worship into immoral worship. They began to worship Baal which included temple prostitution and sexual rites. Baal was the Canaanite god of fertility. They were forsaking the God of their fathers and serving other gods.

"Anything that we choose to do that is contrary to the ways of God is departing from Him and serving other gods."

Anything that we choose to do that is contrary to the ways of God is departing from Him and serving other gods. For instance, we know that God's Word, the Bible is our guidebook for life. In it are instructions and guidance to live a life pleasing to Him. We could start with the Ten Commandments. That is as easy a place to start as any. Most people, even if they don't believe in God, think that obeying the Ten Commandments is a good way to live. The law of the land agrees with some of this thinking as it is against the law to kill, to steal, etc.

Exodus chapter 20 gives us the Ten Commandments. The first two verses say:

> "And God spoke all these words, saying, "I am the LORD your God, who brought you out of the land of Egypt, out of the house of bondage. You shall have no other gods before Me." (Exodus 20:2-3)

What do these words mean to you? What do you think it means to have another god before God? I can give you some examples from my own life to help get you thinking. During the years that I wondered away from God, I partook of many of the things the world had to offer. I drank, slept around, experimented with different drugs, was wasteful with my money, and was basically very selfish. I was raised in church as a little girl and knew better. During my teenage years, I allowed different situations to start to erode my relationship with God. I was looking for love in all the wrong places, as they say. I ran from God from the age of 17 to the age of 39. Twenty-two years on the run but God was patiently waiting for me as He is with you right now.

"I want to encourage you that God has seen all of your tears, has been there through all of your pain, and wants to heal you from the damage that's been done."

I did not fit in with the crowd. I was different. I used to look in the mirror and call myself, "fat, flat, and ugly." So, with that perception of myself, I felt I had to do all the "cool" things just to fit in. What I didn't realize is that it never really made me fit in. It just helped me to spiral downhill with the rest of the crowd. Fortunately, I had praying parents and a praying grandmother. I attribute being alive today because of their prayers.

What about you? Can you look at your life and see how you have gotten where you are? Can you be honest and take a close inventory of the choices and decisions that have helped bring you to this place?

Every life has its ups and downs. We all experience good and bad times. Perhaps your story is so painful you feel as though you will never rebound. I want to encourage you that God has seen all of your tears, has been there through all of your pain, and wants to heal you from the damage that's been done. *He wants to rescue you right where you are.* The beginning of this rescue comes when we admit that we have hit bottom and there is no place else to look but up. We have to look up into the face of Jesus and believe by faith He is there to help us.

There is no one that He doesn't want to rescue. There are no ashes that He doesn't want to turn into beauty. You are beautiful to Him no matter what you think about yourself. You have worth. You are worth the world to Him, so much so that He came to die for you. How many of these "other gods" that we serve are willing to die for us? None. You know that as well as I do.

Would that street dealer die for us? How about that pimp or that guy we hook up with for a night out? Of course not. We are lucky if they remember our names in the morning. Am I getting real here? This is what it takes to set us free. Remember? The truth will set us free. (John 8:32, 36)

The truth is that these "other gods;" sex, drugs, and rock-n-roll will not die for us but could be the very things that kill us.

Write down the ways you feel you have left God for other gods. Be specific. Be honest. It can only help you. Let's pray before you do.

"Jesus, help me to see the ways in which I have walked away from You. Help me to know how I have committed spiritual adultery in my life. I want to come back to You and serve You. I do not want to serve other gods anymore. I am sorry I have walked away from You and ask You to forgive me. Thank you for never leaving my side and bringing me back to you."

If you want to, you can just list some things that come to mind or write a letter to Jesus and talk to Him about it. Whichever way works for you, He is waiting to receive you with open arms. Feel free to take as long as you want with this. There is no need to hurry. Many of us have quite a few things to take care of and we need the time to ponder our lives. The Lord is not in a hurry. He wants to help you. Give yourself the time it takes. You won't be sorry. Use extra paper if you need to.

_____
_____
_____
_____
_____
_____
_____

This is what I call evicting the false gods, the other gods. Have you ever or do you know anyone who has ever been evicted from their apartment or home? Eviction in Webster's Dictionary puts it like this; to force out; expel, eject. Just think about it- you are the landlord and you place an eviction notice on the door of your heart and these other gods are no longer allowed to live in there. How many eviction notices do you need to write today?

Whatever is controlling you instead of the love of Jesus, send it on its way...

Use this as a sample:

I, _____ evict you _____ from my life in Jesus' name and command you to leave. You _____are no longer welcome in my "house" and I serve you notice today. No, not a 30 day notice, an immediate notice. You must leave right now in Jesus' name. I slam the door behind you and lock it from the inside. Jesus has taken up residence in your place and put a padlock of His love on my heart's door. If you try to return, you will be trespassing on Jesus' property and will be found guilty in heaven's court. You will have no appeal and the Mighty Judge will throw you in prison forever where you cannot touch me.

The Bible tells us this is so in Revelation 12:10:

> "Then I heard a loud voice saying in heaven, 'Now salvation, and strength, and the kingdom of our God, and the power of His Christ have come, for the accuser of our brethren, who accused them before our God day and night, has been cast down.' "

Before we move on,

Write as many eviction notices as you need to...

CHAPTER 6
"Mending Brokenness"

"...Let the little children come to Me'
and do not forbid them..."
"And he took them up in His arms
laid His hands on them,
and blessed them."
Mark 10: 14, 16

Now that you have evicted your unauthorized tenants and changed the locks on your heart, you can breathe a sigh of relief. You are being cleansed and given the ability to see things differently. Remember, we said at the beginning that there is a purpose and plan for your life and right now it may not seem so, but this is the place you really need to be.

Moving on, we will be reading Hosea 2:2-3. There is more I want to share with you about these unauthorized tenants. Pay attention as you read and see if you don't recognize yourself in the story.

> "Bring charges against your mother, bring charges; For she is not My wife nor am I her Husband! Let her put away her harlotries from her sight, and her adulteries from between her breasts; Lest I strip her naked And expose her as in the day she was born, And make her like a wilderness, And set her like a dry land, And slay her with thirst."

Here we see that walking away from God produces bad things. We get exposed, stripped naked, and we suffer the consequences of our actions. We need to take a look at the decisions we have made and realize that it is very possible that much of what we are experiencing we have brought upon ourselves. We have done this by walking away from God's path and following our own. Don't you agree?

> **"As we admit our part in our dilemma, we are set free from self-pity and find that we are able to determine in our hearts that we want to change."**

As we admit our part in our dilemma, we are set free from self-pity and find that we are able to determine in our hearts that we want to change. Sometimes looking at ourselves and our situations through a microscope is not a bad thing. We are then able to see the hidden things that have caused us and others so much pain.

Take a moment to reflect on what we have just read in Hosea. Do you feel exposed and naked by being locked up? What do you think it means to be made like a wilderness and be slain with thirst? How do you see these things in your life now? Write your thoughts here. We will be discussing the wilderness later.

_____
_____
_____
_____
_____
_____
_____
_____
_____
_____
_____
_____

Let's now move on to verses 4 and 5 of Hosea 2:

> "I will not have mercy on her children,
> For they are the children of harlotry.
> For their mother has played the harlot;
> She who conceived them has behaved shamefully.
> For she said, "I will go after my lovers,
> Who give me my bread and my water,
> My wool and my linen,
> My oil and my drink."

At first glance this seems very harsh. But let's take a closer look. Think about it this way. We know that if we drink or use drugs while pregnant, our children may be born with defects or addictions. Medical science has proven that to be true through years of study. Many of our children wander around aimlessly without a good foundation because of the things we have chosen to do. Here in the book of Hosea we see that God's people have gone after other things in His place and their children are suffering.

Has that happened in your life or in the lives of anyone you know? Let's pause here for a moment because I want to give you time to talk to God about your life and your children's lives.

Are your children suffering now because of some of the decisions you have made? Is there anything you want to get off your chest before we move on? Take this time to talk to God about your children. Perhaps you would like to write your children a letter. Whatever you choose to do now will affect their lives. *Believe God wants to change the situation with your children and wants to forgive you for any bad decisions you have made concerning them.* Use the following lines to express yourself:

_____

_____

_____

_____

_____

_____

_____

If you have suffered an abortion, I would like to allow you the time right now to talk to God about it and receive His healing forgiveness.

I do not want to move on from here in a hurry. I think that perhaps for many of us, this exercise may be extremely painful. I want to let you rest for awhile before we move on. *I want to assure you that God loves you even though you have made some terrible mistakes.* I want to reassure you that the journey we are on, although painful at times, is going to end up positive. I need to remind you that the truth is setting you free and the more truthful you are with yourself and God, the better your relationships with others will be, especially your children.

Pause - Reflect - Meditate

Take a deep breath. Breathe in. Breathe out. Relax. Do this five times.

Imagine yourself sitting in a park on a warm spring day. You can hear the birds singing and feel the warm air moving past your face. In the distance you hear children playing. Their laughter moves you. Their innocence is something you long for. You want to play just as a child without a care in the world.

I have great news for you! That's exactly what God wants for you. He wants you to be able right now, right where you are, to feel like a carefree child. He wants you to be able to rest in the knowledge that He cares for you more than you will ever know. His arms are outstretched for you to come to Him and rest. Let Him embrace you as His special child as we move along in our study.

CHAPTER 7
"Dust in the Wind"

"...Yes, I have loved you with
an everlasting love;
Therefore with lovingkindness
I have drawn you."
Jeremiah 31:3

In the midst of correction, God is right by our side. He is watching over us every minute. His correction is His love for us so that we don't continue as we are and end up self-destructing. Always remember, if God be for us who can be against us? (Romans 8:31)

What mother, when seeing her young child heading for a hot stove wouldn't stop her? Perhaps you have been heading for a stove with all four burners on high and you were ready to lay down on it. Maybe you were ready to dive into a swimming pool at the deep end from the high dive but there was no water in the pool. Whatever caused you to get locked up, I want to let you know that God never once lost sight of you and has allowed you to be put right where you are so that He can save you from yourself!

Have you ever considered that the very officers that came to pick you up might have been sent by God to pluck you up out of the streets to save your life? Did you ever think that God saw something ahead that you couldn't so He removed you before it happened? Once again, it is a matter of perspective when we are talking about the events that happen in our lives.

Read the following verses from Jeremiah 31:2-4 and ask God to make the words real to you as you read. Substitute your name in the place where it is written, "Israel" and think about what this means for you. Think about *being locked up* as the place of your wilderness.

"...The people who have survived the sword
Found grace in the wilderness---
Israel, when I went to give him rest."
The Lord has appeared of old to me saying;
'Yes, I have loved you with an everlasting love;
Therefore with lovingkindness I have drawn you.
Again I will build you, and you shall be rebuilt,
O virgin of Israel!
You shall again be adorned with your tambourines,
And shall go forth in the dances of those who rejoice."(Jeremiah 31:2-4)

What do you think God is promising you as you read this for yourself?

_____
_____
_____
_____
_____
_____
_____
_____
_____

This is God's promise to us. As we find His grace in our wilderness, we come to the conclusion that God is for us and not against us. We realize that His correction and discipline are truly His love for us. As we read the Bible and learn more about God and His ways, we realize that He is not like us! He does not give up on us easily like we do each other. He continues to woo us, to call us, and to draw us to Himself.

With that truth in our spirits, and the promise that no matter where we have come from or where we find ourselves right now, let us revisit Hosea 2:5 knowing He is ready and willing to accept us back time and time again.

"For their mother has played the harlot;
She who conceived them has behaved shamefully.
For she said, 'I will go after my lovers,
Who give me my bread and my water,
My wool and my linen, My oil and my drink.'"

Here we see one reason for our downfall. We have gone after *our lovers*. We have looked to people, places, and things instead of to God to fulfill our desires. We have committed ourselves to these other lovers instead of God and His ways in our lives. We have turned our backs on God and said *we* can do this thing, we have all we need, and we don't need God. What and who are the other lovers in your life? Is it theft because you don't have enough money to buy the latest fashions, or does stealing satisfy a need to do something risky? Do you write bad checks to get things you can't afford? How about peddling stuff for drugs? Is your latest lover someone you aren't married to? Is he/she promising you the world to get your body? Are you in love with "Jack," my old time friend, "Daniels" or any one of his relatives, "Tequila," Bud," or "Sherry?" Is it uppers, downers, crack cocaine, or prescription drugs?

> **"We have chased all manner of things that in the end do not satisfy. They are like dust in the wind. "**

I could go on but you get the idea. We have chased all manner of things that in the end *do not satisfy*. They are like dust in the wind. Have you ever watched a swirl of dust on a windy day? The dirt is taken up, thrown about, and disappears before our eyes. These *other lovers* may give us instant gratification, but like *dust in the wind*, are gone in a flash leaving us empty and disillusioned.

What and who are your other lovers?
Why do you think you are chasing them?
What are you running from?

Fill in the blanks below as you think of your answers. Remember the truth will set you free. I have filled in the first one from my life to give you an idea. Remember God is for us not against us...

LOVER	REASON	PAIN I'M TRYING TO AVOID
alcohol	fit in/cover up insecurity	rejection

I understand that this exercise may open up some things you do not want to deal with right now and that is ok. I just wanted to let you know you have the option of doing this at any time. It is a simple way to look at your life and try to make some sense of why you do the things you do. I encourage you to continue looking over this list and add things as they come to your mind.

God has told us in the Bible that He loves us with an everlasting love. That means that His love had no beginning and has no end. It is from eternity past, right now, and eternity future. It is something we cannot understand with the human mind. Most of us have been hurt, mistreated, abandoned, and many other things by people we were supposed to be able to trust. This makes it hard for us to comprehend the vastness of God's love for us.

It is the love of God we are searching for. It is God's love that will fill every void in our hearts. Our other lovers are imposters who can't come up with the goods. They are dust in the wind; they are nothing but dust in the wind.

Don't give in to those other lovers any longer. Embrace true love that will not disappear leaving you empty and disillusioned. Embrace the love of God. Do it today. Reach out and embrace Him now.

He's waiting...

CHAPTER 8
"I Still Haven't Found What I'm Looking For"

"Do not lay up for yourselves treasures on earth, where moth and rust destroy and where thieves break in and steal; but lay up for yourselves treasures in heaven, where neither moth nor rust destroys and where thieves do not break in and steal. For where your treasure is, there your heart will be also."
Matthew 6:19-21

In the last chapter, we decided that our other lovers were nothing but dust in the wind. They come and go leaving a trail of pain and suffering behind. We decided to name them and bring the darkness out into the light where they can be exposed. We have taken another step in our journey of letting the truth set us free.

Now we are going to move onto a larger portion of Hosea chapter 2. We want to read verses 6-13. As we do, I'd like to ask you to compare these verses with your own life. Ask God to open your eyes to see yourself in here. Keep your thoughts close by as we will be writing them out at the end of the chapter. You may want to jot them down on a separate piece of paper so you don't forget.

Hosea 2:6-13:

"Therefore, behold, I will hedge up your way with thorns, and wall her in, So that she cannot find her paths. She will chase her lovers, But not overtake them; Yes, she will seek them, but not find them.

Then she will say, 'I will go and return to my first husband. For then it was better for me than now.' For she did not know That I gave her grain, new wine, and oil, and multiplied her silver and gold-- Which they prepared for Baal.

Therefore I will return and take away My grain in its time And My new wine in its season, And will take back My wool and My linen, given to cover her nakedness. Now I will uncover her lewdness in the sight of her lovers, And no one shall deliver her from My hand. I will also cause all her mirth to cease, Her feast days, Her New Moons, Her Sabbaths-- All her appointed feasts. And I will destroy her vines and her fig trees, Of which she has said, 'These are my wages that my lovers have given me.' So I will make them a forest, And the beasts of the field shall eat them. I will punish her For the days of the Baals to which she burned incense. She decked herself with her earrings and jewelry, And went after her lovers but Me she forgot," says the Lord."

This sounds hopeless, don't you think? It seems as though God has all but written her off. He tells her in verse 6, *"I will hedge up your way with thorns, and wall her in so that she cannot find her paths."*

Does this sound like jail or prison? It does to me.

Take a minute to meditate on this asking God to reveal to you how it relates to your life. Write out your thoughts:

_____

_____

_____

_____

_____

I'd like to look deeper into verse seven. Let's read it again.

"She will chase her lovers but not overtake them. Yes, she will seek them, but not find them. Then she will say, "I will go and return to my first husband, for then it was better for me than now."

After running to everything and everyone else, she realizes that it is God that her heart longs for. She decides to return! We are no different. We find out that all of our searching is in vain. We get hooked on this and that. We develop relationships that we know are destructive. We connive, lie, cheat, steal, and manipulate to get our own way. We become addicted to all sorts of things and people. Along the way, we realize we don't even know who we are anymore. We keep looking for something but we never find it. Our hearts are empty. The desire to be satisfied is never met. We grope in the darkness lost and alone. We are so blinded that we don't realize it is God we are searching for.

As we look deeper into Hosea 2:8-13, we see that God has come to the conclusion that He has to intervene in the situation to bring His beloved back to Himself.

As we see ourselves in this description, we are able to realize that God has come into our situation to do what is necessary to bring us back to Himself. Remember me telling you earlier that God's correction is His love for us? Even though it might not feel that way right now, know that God's love has stopped you in your tracks to keep you from self-destructing.

Read it again with me:

> "For she did not know That I gave her grain, new wine, and oil And multiplied her silver and gold-- which they prepared for Baal. Therefore I will return and take away My grain in its time and My new wine in its season, And will take back My wool and My linen, Given to cover her nakedness. Now I will uncover her lewdness in the sight of her lovers, and no one shall deliver her from My hand. I will also cause all her mirth to cease. Her feast days, Her New Moons, Her Sabbaths-- All her appointed feasts. And I will destroy her vines and her fig trees, Of which she has said, 'These are the wages that my lovers have given me.' So I will make them a forest, And the beasts of the field shall eat them. I will punish her For the days of the Baals to which she burned incense. She decked herself with her earrings and jewelry, And went after her lovers, But Me she forgot," says the Lord."

"I believe that as you read this, the Holy Spirit will bring to your mind times you have gone your own way and lost things in the process."

Where do we fit into all this? How do our life stories relate? I believe that as you read this, the Holy Spirit will bring to your mind times you have gone your own way and lost things in the process. Do not dismiss God's prompting to you right now. His discipline is His love for you. Remember us talking about the hot stove earlier?

There is something I want to point out to you about the transition between verses seven and eight. Verse 8 says:

"For she did not know that I gave her grain, new wine, and oil, and multiplied her silver and gold which they prepared for Baal."

Here we see that everything she needed for life was given to her by God. She did not understand His ways so she offered herself to *other lovers*. Not only did she do that, but she gave *them* credit for her satisfaction. In the midst of all her running around and carrying on, God says, "*Me she forgot.*"

This describes me for many years. I was running around, hiding behind drugs, alcohol, and men. I came up short every time. The more I lived in the fog of make believe, the lonelier I got. How about you? When the party is over and the hangover subsides, what are you left with?

Have you walked away from God because you couldn't see past the things going on in your life? Have you walked away not understanding that He really cares for you and wants to supply your needs? Have you turned to other people, places and things? Have you forgotten Him?

Take some time right now to examine your life. Who have you looked to for comfort? What have you chased in order to get relief? Where have you gone to find peace of mind? What are the things you wished you could get rid of so that you could start over and experience the life Jesus died to give you? Please take as much time as you need and allow God to make Himself real to you.

_____

_____

_____

_____

_____

_____

_____

_____

_____

_____

We are all on a search for meaning in life. We are special to God and He created us with a void in our hearts that only He can fill. Until we evict those other lovers like we have talked about, we will walk around saying, "*I still haven't found what I'm looking for.*" We will continue to look for love in all the wrong places. We will come up short and empty every time.

CHAPTER 9
"Switching Sides"

"For once you were full of darkness,
but now you have light from the Lord.
So live as people of light! For this light
within you produces only what is
good and right and true."
Ephesians 5:8-9 (Life Recovery Bible)

I believe God has plucked you out of the streets to save your life. I believe He has allowed you to be placed where you are so that you can hear Him calling you back to Himself. I believe that no matter how hopeless your situation seems right now, that He has a plan for you. I believe that as we continue to look at the book of Hosea you will find meaning in all the madness.

Before we move on, I would like to give you an opportunity to re-read the list you made in chapter seven. Go ahead and add anything you may have forgotten. If you want to ask God to help you remove these "other gods" from your life, pray with me right now.

"Lord Jesus, I recognize that in and of myself I do not have the ability to change and, if I am honest, I may not even want to. But, by Your Holy Spirit, I believe You are here with me and want to help me. I am tired of living the kind of life I have been living and need Your help right now. I present this list to You knowing that You already know my heart and what I am capable of.

I ask You to help me be the person You want me to be. I ask You to bring people into my life who can help me. I give You all my hurts, wounds, mistakes, and desires. I ask You to help me desire You more than any person, place, or thing. I believe that You love me and want the best for me. I give you all I am right now and trust myself into Your care. In Your precious Son Jesus' name. Amen."

If you have prayed that prayer with me, believe in faith that God heard you and is overjoyed at your response! Believe with me that He will help you do the things you asked Him to help you do. Believe that your life can change.

> **"***I am so proud of you for coming this far because I'm sure it hasn't been easy at times.***"**

I am so proud of you for coming this far because I'm sure it hasn't been easy at times. Some of the things we have looked at have been very personal and painful. You may have wanted to take the easy way out or even quit. You might have been tempted to give in and say this could never work for you. BUT YOU DIDN'T!

I can relate because I struggle every day with the same kind of negative thoughts. These types of thoughts are lies that come from none other than the devil. He does not want you to put your trust in God. He is not happy about losing his grip on you. He has had you for so long that he's got you thinking that you can never change. He has called you names, beat you up for failing, and all the while it was him tempting you, playing you into his hands.

He is a liar, a cheat, and the Bible says he has come to kill us, steal from us, and destroy us. Do you believe that is true? Has He not killed your hopes and dreams and stolen from you? Has he not tempted you to do things that could ultimately destroy you? Of course he has. He is called a thief in the Bible. Yes, he is the conniving thief whose whole mission is to steal from us and to destroy us.

Jesus is the one who calls him a thief and tells us what his mission is in John 10:10. He says, *"The thief does not come except to steal, and to kill, and to destroy..."* That settles it for me. If Jesus says it, it has to be true. What are your thoughts about that? Can you take a minute and look at your life and have the courage to put down on paper the things that have been stolen from you? Can you see past the lies of the devil and expose him for what he has done to you? Will you write out your thoughts about how he has come to kill you, steal from you, and destroy you? Will you take responsibility for your part in his plan?

Again, these are hard things to look at. I realize this. I want to give you all the time you need with this exercise because it can be a painful one. But I want to assure you that just as there is great pain in childbirth, when it is over, the joy swallows up the pain. I promise you, we are heading for that joy. Stick with me.

In the space provided, I am asking you to list what you have lost because of your part in the devil's plan for your life. I am asking you to be totally honest, not pointing the finger at others, but seeking the truth. I know this may produce some intense feelings of grief and sorrow. Let the tears flow *knowing that God is right here with you to catch them.*

Did you know your tears are important to God? They are so important that He catches them and saves them. Remember what we have been saying all along, *"If God be for us, who can be against us?* (Romans 8:31)

Before you begin your list, I would like for you to read Psalm 56:8-9:

> "You remember my wanderings;
> Put my tears into Your bottle;
> Are they not in Your book?
> When I cry out to You,
> Then my enemies will turn back;
> This I know because God is for me."

Re- read Psalm 56:8-9 a few times. Ask God to allow you to feel Him close to you. Ask Him to catch the tears as they fall. Let Him love you as you write. *Let Him embrace you as you get real with yourself.* Take as much time as you need.

_____
_____
_____
_____
_____
_____
_____
_____
_____
_____
_____
_____
_____
_____
_____
_____
_____
_____
_____

Now that you have completed this exercise, I want to pray for you.

Dear Jesus, would You help my friend understand that even if the devil has a plan to kill, steal, and destroy her life, that You also have a plan? Will You help her see the plan You have and that You are more powerful in her life than the devil? Will You bring hope and peace right now where there is hopelessness and strife? Will You bring joy and laughter where there is sorrow and fear? Will You come to my friend right now and comfort her with Your great love? I ask this in Your precious name and for Your glory. Amen.

> **❝***Although the devil has certainly played us as fools, our lives can turn around. We can truly experience life the way God intended and that is to live in relationship with Him.***❞**

Before we move on I want to share something with you. There is good news in the rest of what Jesus was saying in John 10:10. Yes, He did say that the thief does not come except to steal, and to kill, and to destroy. But He continues speaking and says, "*... I have come that they may have life, and that they may have it more abundantly.*"

This is the good news, my dear friend! Although the devil has certainly played us as fools, *our lives can turn around.* We can truly experience life the way God intended and that is to live life in relationship with Him. As we move toward that abundant life Jesus is speaking about, we move away from the life the devil has duped us into living. We are moving from darkness to light, from death to life. Ownership is being changed from the devil to God. The devil is losing his grip on us as we learn of God and start believing His Word.

He (the devil) does not give up without a fight. But we have weapons to win the fight at our disposal if we will learn to use them. In this study of Hosea, I believe we are learning things about ourselves and God that are more powerful than all the devil can come up with. Once again, it is the truth that is setting us free. Free from what? From the devil's grip on our lives. In the next session, we will be heading back to Hosea, the second chapter and to one of my favorite passages. It will reveal to us *the extraordinarily, intense, immense love God has for us.* It will show us how we can look at our situations differently. It will give us a better understanding of what is happening to us. *We will find hope in the midst of our crisis.*

We have changed sides my friend! We are no longer on the losing side accepting the fate of a loser, but we are on the winning side learning to live like a winner!

CHAPTER 10
"Tasting Hope"

"O Lord my God, I cried out to
You and You healed me.
O Lord, You brought my soul
up from the grave;
You have kept me alive,
that I should not go down to the pit.
Sing praise to the Lord, you saints of His,
And give thanks at the remembrance
of His holy name.
For His anger is but for a moment,
His favor is for life;
Weeping may endure for a night,
But joy comes in the morning.
Psalm 30:2-5

I have given this chapter the title "Tasting Hope" because that is what I want for you right now. I want you to *taste hope* knowing that you are not alone and that God has not forgotten you. As a matter of fact, He is right here with you and wants you to know just how much you are loved and cared for. He is just a prayer away.

Did you know that prayer is not something you have to muster up and say big important words? Did you know that you can pray without words? Prayer is a two way conversation between your spirit and God's. You have probably been praying without words the whole time you were doing the exercises in this book. I want you to know God has never left your side.

Remember what He said to us earlier in Jeremiah 31:3-4? I will write it out again here for you:

"The LORD has appeared of old to me saying; "Yes, I have loved you with an everlasting love; Therefore with loving-kindness I have drawn you. Again I will build you, and you shall be rebuilt, O virgin of Israel! You shall again be adorned with your tambourines, And shall go forth in the dances of those who rejoice."

He is telling us that even though our lives have become shattered, He has called us back to Himself and His intention is to help us rebuild. His promise here is that when we partner up with Him in the rebuilding of our lives, we will rejoice. This is the taste of hope. It is the anticipation that things will turn around because God is for us and not against us.

"Oh, taste and see that the LORD is good;
Blessed is the man who trusts in Him!" (Psalm 34:8)

THIS IS THE TASTE OF HOPE-
HE PROMISES TO REBUILD YOUR SHATTERED LIFE.

Trust Him to rebuild your life.

So far we have examined our lives and taken a hard look at ourselves. We have tried to be as honest as we can. We have written down some things we haven't shared with anyone. We have talked to God in ways we never did before. We have begun to trust, even if just a bit. We are changing. We are learning more every day. We are not where we want to be, but we are not where we used to be. Thank God for His care and His Holy Spirit that is enabling us to do this!

We have come to realize that we have played a part in the things the devil had planned for us. We have learned that we've been chasing everything under the sun except God. We have repented, prayed, and asked God for His forgiveness. We have looked at the character of God and found that He is disciplining us. We have read that He disciplines those that He loves.

Now we are going to move on and get a better understanding of this place of discipline that we will call *our wilderness.*

Let us resume our journey:

Read with me Hosea 2:14:

"Therefore, behold, I will allure her,
Will bring her into the wilderness,
And speak comfort to her."

This is incredible! Did you get that? If not, read it again, and again. God is saying to her that because of her unfaithfulness, all of her chasing other gods, all of her running and debauchery, He is going to allure her and bring her to a place where *He will speak comfort to her.* Will you listen for His comfort in the midst of your crisis? Will you take a few minutes and thank Him that He has never left your side? Be still and know He is God. *Be still and rest in His love for you.*

Pause - Reflect - Relax - Meditate

During our study of Hosea, we are learning more about God and ourselves. If we are honest, we will admit we are much like the people in the story. We have drifted from Him and He wants to bring us back. The only problem with that is the way He goes about it.

Have we found ourselves in this situation because we have forgotten God? Have we gotten so caught up in all the drama that we can never see a way out? *If so, we are in a good place.* If we see His discipline as His love for us *we will have hope.* If we look at the things we have lost because of our choices, we will be better equipped to move forward with our lives and do the right thing. If we understand what He is doing while we are locked up, *we can have peace* knowing there is a purpose for everything and our misery will end one day.

> **"*If we see His discipline as His love for us we will have hope.*"**

Let's take a closer look at some of these words in Hosea 2:14. Let's examine the word, *therefore* first. *Therefore* is a word that's used as a bridge here. It takes us from one thought and connects us to the next. God has seen the condition of His people (us) and knows the only way they (we) will listen and come back to Him is if He intervenes in their (our) lives.

Because He loves us so much and desires an intimate relationship with us, at times He has to put our lives on hold. He has to slow us down, sit us down, and place us in the position where we have nothing to distract us from His voice.

Remember, the whole chapter before verse fourteen tells us why God is doing what He is doing and then verse fourteen begins to tell us how. He says in Hosea 2:14 that He is alluring us and bringing us into our wilderness so that He can speak comfort to us.

Think about this for a minute. When we are locked up, we're told when to get up, when to eat, when to go to bed. We no longer have the luxury to choose what to wear, what to watch on TV, or what we eat. We have lost all rights to most decision making. We go through the motions day by day without any responsibility except to do what they tell us to do.

This may be true, but there is one decision that can never be taken away from us. That's the decision we make about how we are going to spend our time. Are we going to sit around wasting it riding an emotional roller coaster or are we going to look at it from God's point of view? If we look at it from God's point of view, we will see value in what is happening and come out of it a better person.

God says that He is taking His unfaithful one (us) and alluring her (us) and bringing her (us) to the wilderness to speak comfort to her (us). We are locked up. We are in the wilderness. We can expect to be comforted.

"I believe you are where you are right now because God wants to show you His love. It may not seem like it to you, but I assure you His love will bring you comfort if you will let it. "

I believe you are where you are right now because God wants to show you His love. It may not seem like it to you, but I assure you His love will bring you comfort if you will let it. *Remember, God is for you not against you*, especially in the wilderness.

As we look at two words here, *allure* and *wilderness*, I want you to think about your current situation and how God is doing this very thing in your life.

Allure means to attract by fascination, to charm. The Life Recovery Bible says it this way, "*But I will win her back once again. I will lead her out into the desert and speak tenderly to her there.*"

Copy the words from the Life Recovery Bible on the lines below then meditate on them for a few minutes. Read them at least five times slowly. "But I will win her back once again. I will lead her out into the desert and speak tenderly to her there." Believe this for yourself. He is talking about you. Can you feel Him near? Ask Him to reveal His love to you.

_____

_____

_____

_____

Now, ask God to show you how this applies to your life right now. Then, write what you believe He has shown you.

_____

_____

_____

_____

_____

Let's take a look at the words wilderness and desert for a moment. In the Bible, the desert is not a pleasant place to be. It is any desolate and unpopulated area. It means unsettled land. It is a dangerous place because if you are caught in the wilderness, you could encounter wild animals or hostile tribesmen. You would be facing these things without support of community. You would be out there all alone facing life in danger with little around you but rocks, hot sun, and burning sand. It is a place of desolation and desperation. No water, food, or comfort. It is a land of infertility where nothing grows.

Read what David writes in Psalm 63:1:

> "O GOD, You are my God;
> Early will I seek You;
> My soul thirsts for You;
> My flesh longs for You
> In a dry and thirsty land
> Where there is no water."

Here we can visualize David out in the desert, the wilderness with nothing. There is nothing to eat, no water to drink. He is without hope. Here David cries out, "God, You are my God."

He recognizes God. He calls out to Him and tells Him his situation. He calls for help. He is in the desert. He recognizes the state of his soul. He is thirsty, thirsty for the Living God. He says his body longs for God. He is not longing for the things of this world. He is longing for that which will satisfy his soul. He is longing for God.

In Psalm 42:1-5 we read more of the same. Meditate on these words as you read them considering your own desert and wilderness.

Again, from the Life Recovery Bible:

> "As the deer longs for streams of water,
> So I long for you, O God.
> I thirst for God, the living God.
> When can I go and stand before Him?
> Day and night I have only tears for food,
> While my enemies continually taunt me, saying,
> "Where is this God of yours?"
> My heart is breaking
> As I remember how it used to be.

> I walked among the crowds of worshipers
> Leading a great procession to the house of God,
> Singing for joy and giving thanks
> Amid the sound of a great celebration!
> Why am I discouraged?
> Why is my heart so sad?
> I will put my hope in God!
> I will praise Him again--
> My Savior and my God!"

Here we read that in the midst of great anguish, the author is crying out to God. Did you know it takes humility to cry out to God? In reality we must lay down our pride, our self-sufficiency, and our own plans to ask for God's help. We cannot come to Him with bargaining. We cannot hide our hearts from Him because He knows every thought before we think it. We must come to a place of surrender. Are you ready to surrender? As we cry out to God and place our trust in His goodness, we can lay hold of hope.

The author of Psalm 42 asks, "Why am I discouraged? Why is my heart so sad? I will put my hope in God! I will praise Him again- my Savior and my God!" This is an act of his will. He says, "I will!"

Will you put your hope in God today? Will you praise Him today? Will you speak to your soul and say "Why are you so discouraged? Why are you so sad?" As you meditate on these things, write yourself a letter. Then write a letter of praise to God for hearing your cries.

_____

_____

_____

_____

_____

_____

_____

_____

_____

_____

_____

CHAPTER 11
"Prisoner of Hope"

"Return to the stronghold,
You prisoners of hope.
Even today I declare
That I will restore double to you."
Zechariah 9:12

As we begin this next session, let's go to the Lord in prayer.

Dear Jesus, I have come so far. I have decided to give faith a try and taste hope even when I am feeling down. I am moving forward believing that You cannot lie and that Your Word is truth. I see by this verse that You are calling me a "Prisoner of Hope." I don't know what that means but I am willing to learn. Please help me to understand what You are trying to teach me about myself and my situation. Please help me to retain what I am learning so that when I need it, I will re-member. I need You in my life and trust You with it. Be close to me now as I continue. Your friend,

_____.

What does it mean to be a prisoner of hope? Well, if you are locked up, you surely know what it means to be a prisoner. Let's get into the Bible and see what it says about this. The definition of hope in the Bible is bit different than what most of us are familiar with. Hope in the Bible can be defined as confident expectation. It is not wishful thinking.

Let's say for instance, your visit time is approaching and your friends or family members have not been to see you in awhile. Wishful thinking says to you, *"Well I hope someone comes today. I hope they don't disappoint me again."* Or, when mail call is announced, you think, *I hope I get a letter today.* These are wishful thinking thoughts that may or may not have any faith attached to them.

The type of hope we are talking about in this verse is a confident expectation that what God says is the truth. Once again, we can look to the Bible to determine what is true. In Titus 1:2 it says simply that God cannot lie. Hope and truth go together when we are talking about God and what He says.

So what does it mean to be a *prisoner of hope?* Here is what I think. When I think about what it means to be *locked up*, I imagine a place where I cannot come and go as I please because the whole place is under security for the protection of all who are there. I think about a place where my decision making has come to a halt because the decisions I have made have not been very good. I see a place where my rights have been removed from me because using them freely has caused me and others harm. I see this as a place where I have to learn to respect others as well as myself. I suppose it to be a place where I have time to reflect, regroup, and get myself together so that I can live the abundant life Jesus died to give me.

That is what I envision being "*locked up* to be. But what about the Bible? What is God saying here when he calls us *prisoners of hope?*

What do you think it means? _____

_____

_____

_____

I want to be *locked up* at all times with God's truth about everything. Being *locked up* in this sense is a very safe place to be because if I am *locked up* with God as my officer, the devil can't get to me! If I am in a place where I can't get out that means I will be under God's protection, correction, and education at all times. I will be protected from the devil and all his schemes against me. I will be protected from his lies and have God's truth as my anchor. God will correct me when I need it for my protection as well as others. He will teach me His ways so that I won't follow my own and get myself into trouble.

Remember me telling you to keep notes so that you can go back and be reminded of things that God has spoken to you or that you have felt? As I was writing this chapter I decided Zechariah 9:12 was the verse I wanted to use to begin the chapter. When I opened my Bible to that page, I found some notes that I had written beside it back on September 23, 2006. Here is what I had written:

> This day I release myself from the prison of doubt and place myself as a prisoner of hope. Walk with chains of hope. Christ, in me, my hope. 1 Timothy 1:1

As you can see, those notes written in 2006 were written beside a verse that had special meaning to me that day. I must have been struggling with doubt and feeling hopeless. I received comfort and hope as I read that verse and applied it to my life. You will be surprised at how God will use His Word every time you read it. All you need to do is be open to what He is saying to you through it.

I want to show you some of God's truth about you that you may never have known. I will be listing some verses for you to meditate on and make them your own. God's Word is full of encouraging things for us to learn. Unfortunately we have been listening to the wrong voice for so long that we believe the wrong things. We believe things like, *I'm stupid, I'm dumb, I can't do anything right. I won't ever be able to change. I am not loveable. I am unacceptable. I am ugly inside and out.* I have some verses for you to read that will tell you what God's truth says about these lies. Look them up in your Bible if you have one. Compare them and see if you don't agree with me that it's better to be *a prisoner of hope rather than a prisoner of lies.*

1.) Truth is: I have the mind of Christ. (I Corinthians 2:16)
  Lie is: I'm stupid, I'm dumb.

2.) Truth is: I can do all things through Christ who strengthens me. (Phil 4:13)
  Lie is: I can't do anything right. I won't ever be able to change.

3.) Truth is: God loves me with His love that never ends. (Jeremiah 31:3)
  Lie is: I am unlovable.

4.) Truth is: I am accepted because of Jesus. (Ephesians 1:6)
  Lie is: I am unacceptable.

5.) Truth is: I am beautiful to God. (Psalm 45:13-14)
  Lie is: I am ugly inside and out.

Can you see how knowing what God says about you will help you defeat the devil when he comes knocking at your door? If he can get you to put yourself down, he will step all over you and you will end up doing the things that agree with his lies. Just kick him off your turf with the truth of what God says about you in the Bible.

Jesus did that very thing when the devil was tempting Him in the wilderness! *Even Jesus spent time in the wilderness.* Can you believe the nerve of the devil? He tried to tempt the Son of God! The beauty of that is that Jesus understands what it's like for us. Let's see what the Bible says about Jesus' wilderness.

In Luke 4:1 we read:

> "Then Jesus, being filled with the Holy Spirit, returned from the Jordan and was led by the Spirit into the wilderness..."

How about that? *Jesus was led by the Holy Spirit* into the wilderness, just like we are! That should encourage you. There was a reason and a purpose for Jesus' wilderness. I am certain that it was NOT because God was mad at him. I believe He was sent into the wilderness so He could show us what to do when we entered ours. When He was in the wilderness, hungry and tired, the devil came to tempt Him.

Does that sound familiar? The devil comes when we are weak and hungry, tired, and discouraged. He has a field day when we are most vulnerable. What did Jesus do when the devil invaded His space?

The Bible tells us that three times He told the devil, *"It is written."* And then He quoted verses from the Bible. Jesus, being our perfect example in everything shows us what to do. When we are in the wilderness and the devil comes knocking, we say, *"It is written."* And then speak the Word of God against him. That is why it is so important to know what the Bible says.

"Be encouraged today that the negative thoughts you have about yourself are not the thoughts God has toward you. "

Be encouraged today that the negative thoughts you have about yourself are not the thoughts God has toward you. The more you read the Bible and find out how God sees you, the easier it will be for you to recognize the devil and his lies. You will have victory in your life as you overcome the devil with God's Word.

Start making a list on your own as you read the Bible and find things that God says that will snuff out the devils lies. Share it with others. You will be surprised at how it helps you during your day.

Here is a great one to start your list with:

Jeremiah 29:11:

> "For I know the thoughts that I think toward you, says the LORD, thoughts of peace and not of evil, to give you a future and a hope."

When those negative thoughts about yourself sneak up on you, have this verse ready to counteract them and throw them out.

Jesus said that the Holy Spirit will bring to our remembrance those things that He has taught us. When we learn the truths in the Bible, we may not need them right away, but they get stored in our hearts for when we do. I promise you this is true. It has happened to me many times, including the writing of this book.

John 14:26 says; "But the Helper, the Holy Spirit, whom the Father will send in My name, He will teach you all things, and bring to your remembrance all things that I said to you."

I encourage you to make it a point to learn as much as you can so that you can be strong in the day of battle. God cannot lie. Jesus cannot lie. So if He said He would remind you, He will. Our part is to read and learn. The rest is up to Him.

Jot down some of the negative thoughts you have toward yourself that I haven't discussed and make it a point to learn what God says about them in the Bible. When you come across something that will change your thinking to the way God thinks, write it down.

Let's become *Prisoners of Hope* by learning and believing what God says about us.

CHAPTER 12
"The Voice of Hope"

"Though the Lord gave you adversity for food
and suffering for drink,
he will still be with you to teach you.
You will see your teacher with your own eyes.
Your own ears will hear him.
Right behind you a voice will say,
"This is the way you should go,"
whether to the right or to the left.
Then you will destroy all your silver idols
and your precious gold images.
You will throw them out like filthy rags,
Saying to them, "Good riddance!"
Isaiah 30:20-22
(The Life Recovery Bible)

We are beginning to uncover the lies we have believed that make us feel hopeless, unworthy, and fearful. We are moving away from the "stinkin thinkin." We are learning that the devil has a loud voice and that we have been listening to his voice rather than God's.

Let's take another look at Hosea 2:14:

"Therefore, behold, I will allure her,
Will bring her into the wilderness,
And speak comfort to her."

We are going to spend the next session examining this verse looking to understand the voice of comfort. I invite you to take an inventory of your surroundings. Do you remember what we said a wilderness is?

We learned that a wilderness is a place of hot, dry, waterless wasteland where nothing grows. It is a dangerous place to be alone because you might run into wild animals or vicious tribesmen. It is a place of utter despair, a place of hopelessness.

Think for a minute about where you are. If you were asked to define wilderness by what you are experiencing now, what would your definition be? Place your answer on the following lines. Remember, there is no right or wrong answer, just write what comes from your heart. How do you see your present situation? Who and what are the wild animals and vicious tribesmen? They could be fear, anxiety, depression, guilt, to name a few. They could be anger, hate, or evil thoughts. It could be the loss of control of your life. Whatever or whoever it is, talk to God. Tell Him how you feel. Be Honest. He knows anyway. Remember, it's the truth that will set you free. Face your own demons straight on and see what God will do for you!

_____

_____

_____

_____

_____

Because we have found ourselves in the wilderness, *we can expect to receive comfort from God.* That is what He says in the verse we are studying. He says He will speak comfort to us. Can you think of any time during the time you have been locked up that God might have been trying to speak comfort to you?

Sometimes when we are in a crisis situation, we do not hear or see things clearly. I can promise you that God has not forgotten you; that He has been speaking to you all along even if you haven't been able to hear Him. How do you think God speaks to us?

Let me give you some examples from what I have learned in Moss Justice Center. Men and women in that facility have spent anywhere from a couple days to a couple years waiting for sentencing or rehab beds.

Waiting is the hardest thing, they tell me. The unknown can be very frightening, especially if you find out that those on the outside have decided they don't want anything to do with you. I know it can be weeks before you speak to your lawyer and sometimes they really don't have much to tell you.

It is during these times of waiting that God wants to speak to you. He wants to comfort you while you wait. He wants you to know that He hasn't forgotten you even if everyone else has.

Of course, He will speak to you when you are reading the Bible. Maybe a verse will jump up off the page and you will think, *Man, I get it now!* Perhaps you will be reading a story in the Bible and you feel like you fit right into it and an answer will come to you about something you didn't understand. God loves to speak to us through His Word. But He is not limited in the ways in which He speaks. If He can speak through a donkey as it tells us in Numbers 22:28, He can speak to us in just about any way, don't you think?

Many times as I am ministering in Moss Justice, I see God speaking to the ladies through each other. At times, I have witnessed Him speaking across the room through scripture, songs, or comments. Just at the right time, a lady may have an encouraging word for someone else. Maybe an officer comes in with a positive attitude and greets us with a smile. These are all ways God can speak to us.

Gifts and talents are other things God will use to speak to us. There are so many gifts and talents locked up in these incredible ladies it amazes me. They write music, poetry, sketch drawings, and teach the Word of God. There have been times when I hear someone sing and all I can do is kneel on the floor and worship. It feels as though I am being sung over by an angel.

> **"*We don't have to look far to realize God is speaking. Our problem is that our ears are all plugged up with the wrong voice!*"**

Just the other day, a young lady sang a song she had written while she was on lock down. I can't remember how long they had her on lock down, but this song was incredible. I am not much for rap music, but her song had me going. At the end, I was jumping and yelling, "Yes!" to the powerful thing. It was God speaking. It is hard to remember all the words to a rap song, but the end of the song went like this, "And the first will be last and the last will be first." Her song was called "Surrender." At the end I told her she's got to do something with that talent! We don't have to look far to realize God is speaking. Our problem is that our ears are all plugged up with the wrong voice!

Just recently God wanted to let me know how much He loved me and thought about me. I received a phone call from someone I hadn't spoken to for over three years. It was not that we had an argument or anything like that. We had just lost contact. This person called and told me that God had placed me on her heart. I had just gotten out of the hospital and was recuperating. How special is this God of ours, to remind us of how much we are loved!

God is a God of solutions. His timing is always perfect. At times we believe He is taking forever to do something but when we see His hand at work, we realize He knows what He is doing and we don't have a clue. It is awesome to watch God work in our lives. When we look around and listen, He will always come through and speak to us in ways that boggle our minds.

Jesus made this very clear in John 10:27. He says, *"My sheep hear My voice, and I know them, and they follow Me."* This is you, my dear friend. This is me. We are His sheep and we can hear His voice. All we need to do is be still and listen. (Psalm 46:10)

I want to invite you now to pray with me that God will let you know when He is speaking to you.

Dear Jesus,
I am so thankful that You want to speak to me in my wilderness. I believe You brought me here to help me and to speak comfort to me. I believe I am no different than any of Your other children. I believe You love me every bit as much as You loved them in Hosea's time. I am asking You to help me recognize Your voice of comfort. I ask You to help me respond when I do. Thank You Jesus for listening. Amen.

I would like to encourage you to keep a journal if you can. In this journal, keep a record of the times during the day you believe God is speaking to you and how He does it. Make it a point to open your eyes up to what is going on around you and listen for His voice. The more you listen, the easier it will be to hear Him. Remember though, everything you hear must be judged by the Bible. For instance, if the voice you hear tells you something different than what the Bible says, it's not God speaking.

We are looking to hear the voice of hope while we are in the wilderness. Even when God is disciplining us, He will do it with mercy and grace. *His discipline is not harsh or abusive.* It is always with His tender heart toward you. It is with the same heart that sent Jesus to the cross. It is with the great love of an awesome Creator that wants nothing but the best for His children. Read with me James 2:13:

"...Mercy triumphs over judgment."

This is the voice of Hope in the wilderness

CHAPTER 13
"7 Promises"

"For Jesus Christ, the Son of God,
does not waver between
"Yes" and "No." He is the one
whom Silas, Timothy, and I preached
to you, and as God's ultimate
"Yes," he always does what he says."
2 Corinthians 1:19
(Life Recovery Bible)

We have learned that we can forget God and chase after other lovers. We see that God intervenes in our lives at crucial times so that we are no longer distracted. We then are given the opportunity to return to Him. We have learned that He woos us into our own personal wilderness so that He can speak comfort to us. We have been encouraged to expect good things from our wilderness experience.

Now, I want to focus on the seven promises God has for us while we are in the wilderness. I need to remind you that God is not like us. He does not lie. The Bible tells us in Numbers 23:19 that *"God is not a man, that He should lie..."* We can believe that if He has said something, it is true. We can believe that if God says He brings us into the wilderness to speak comfort to us, then He will.

If we examine our time in the wilderness using Hosea's story and recognize God's heart, *we will have hope.* We will realize that we have not been left out in the cold; that in fact we are right where we need to be. As I said before, God has given us some awesome promises if we will take the time to look behind the scenes.

I want to encourage you to write these promises down on a separate sheet of paper, as well as below. Meditate on them daily so that they become part of who you are. Put them in a place where they are readily available to you if that is possible.

You will be speaking the Word of God over your life instead of the negative things that have plagued you for so long. You will be telling the devil that God has a plan for your life and that you realize you are right where you need to be. You will be making a liar out of the devil and speaking God's truth over yourself. You will be speaking light into your darkness, hope into your hopelessness. It is all part of winning the battle in the wilderness.

Write each promise out on the lines below. Believe they are for you right now where you are:

1.) He will speak comfort to me. Hosea 2:14

_____

2.) I will see purpose and destiny for my life. Hosea 2:15

_____

3.) I will have hope, joy, and freedom from fear. Hosea 2:15

_____

4.) I will no longer be a slave, but a bride. Hosea 2:16--Hosea 2:19-20

_____

5.) I will be set free from my sin and addictions. Hosea 2:17

_____

6.) I will experience peace. Hosea 2:18

_____

7.) I will see new things coming from my life. Hosea 2:21-22

_____

We will be discussing each of these promises in detail as we move on. We will examine our lives in relation to what God is saying in Hosea. We will see His plans and purposes for this time in our lives and in the end we will experience hope in the midst of our crisis.

Remind yourself that God does not lie. Remind yourself that all of these promises are for you. Go back through your notes and re-read what you have written when you believe you heard

God speaking to you. Thank Him for helping you hear His voice and for His comfort. Before we move on, perhaps you would like to write a letter of thanks to God.

_____

_____

_____

_____

_____

_____

_____

_____

_____

_____

_____

_____

_____

_____

_____

_____

_____

_____

_____

_____

_____

_____

_____

_____

_____

_____

_____

CHAPTER 14
"Comfort's Voice"

"Comfort, yes, comfort My people!"
Says your God.
Speak comfort to Jerusalem,
and cry out to her,
That her warfare is ended,
That her iniquity is pardoned;
For she has received from the LORD's hand
Double for all her sins."
The voice of one crying in the wilderness.
"Prepare the way of the LORD;
Make straight in the desert
A highway for our God.
Every valley shall be exalted
And every mountain and hill brought low;
The crooked places shall be made straight
And the rough places smooth;
The glory of the Lord shall be revealed,
And all flesh shall see it together;
For the mouth of the Lord has spoken."
Isaiah 40:1-5

Now we will start to look at the promises of Hosea and discuss them. My intention here is to go deeper into the Bible and help you understand how to apply its truth to your life. We are not doing this merely to gain more information about God or the Bible, but we are searching for meaning in our lives and laying hold of the promises of God.

The first promise we wrote out in the last chapter comes from Hosea 2:14. Here we read God's promise to speak comfort to us in our wilderness.

Let's write it out again to refresh our memories:

He will speak comfort to me. Hosea 2:14

We have already talked about God speaking through the Bible. I want us to look at what the Bible says about itself, comfort, and hope.

Read what Romans 15:4 says,

> "For whatever things were written before were written for our learning, that
> we through the patience and comfort of the Scriptures might have hope."

Here we see the Bible itself says that as we read it, we will receive comfort and hope. For many of us, comfort and hope seem out of reach. Why do you think that is? I have an idea. First, the devil does not want you to believe any of the Bible is for you. He wants you to question everything because it doesn't seem to work for you. He wants you to give up before you start. I know this to be true because he does it to me all the time.

Here is how you battle this thing. You say;

"Devil, you have no right to me or my mind. I believe what the Bible says and I believe it is for me. I believe that God wants to speak comfort to me and bring me hope by reading the Bible. The Bible tells me in James 4:7 that if I submit to God and resist you, you must go. I am submitting my life and my time here to God. I am resisting you and you must get away from me. Be gone in Jesus' name."

Now that we have that settled, let's look at the Bible and read what it says about comfort and hope. I am going to give you two verses. After you have read them, I want you to jot down what they mean to you in your present situation.

Let's pray first.

Dear Jesus, Help me to learn what you are saying to me through these verses. Please make them real to me no matter how I feel or what I am going through. Please remind me of Your love and care as I read Your Word. Thank You for hearing my prayer. Amen.

1Timothy 1:1 "...the Lord Jesus Christ, our hope." _____

_____

_____

_____

Romans 5:5 "Now hope does not disappoint, because the love of God has been poured out in our hearts by the Holy Spirit who was given to us."_____

_____

_____

_____

I would like to point out two things here. First, we must look to Jesus for our hope. He is the only one we can totally rely on to never fail us. He has our best interests in mind no matter what it looks like.

Remember, we said that He sees the whole picture where we only see what is front of us. Secondly, Romans 5:5 says that hope does not disappoint. If Jesus is our hope, then Jesus does not disappoint. Why can Jesus not disappoint? The Bible tells us why. It says because the love of God has been poured out in our hearts by the Holy Spirit who was given to us.

It is when we come to grips with the reality of the perfect, limitless love God has for us, we are able to trust Jesus and rely on Him for our hope. If you are unable to do that, I want to pray with you. I want to ask God to help you see how much He loves you. I cannot teach you that. You cannot make yourself believe it. Only God through His Holy Spirit can shine the light inside of you so that you can see. It is possible to walk through the most trying situations in our lives and *still hold onto the hope* God wants us to have in Him.

> **"***It is when we come to grips with the reality of the perfect, limitless love God has for us, we are able to trust Jesus and rely on Him for our hope.***"**

Dear Jesus, I come to You right now and ask You to help my friend here know from the depths of her being just how much You love her. I am asking You to show her Your love in a very special way. I ask You to help her be able to trust You and experience the hope that You have for her. I ask these things in Your precious name. Amen.

The next passage in the Bible I want to share with you concerning hope comes from the Old Testament in Jeremiah. It is one of my favorites. We read it in a previous chapter. When we talk about this in Moss Justice, the ladies experience hope and their faces light up. They have commented over the years about how this passage in the Bible has given them a new outlook. I believe it will do the same for you.

Jeremiah 29:11-14 (from the Life Recovery Bible)

> "For I know the plans I have for you," says the LORD. "They are plans for good and not for disaster, to give you a future and a hope. In those days when you pray, I will listen. If you look for Me wholeheartedly, you will find Me. I will be found by you," says the Lord. "I will end your captivity and restore your fortunes. I will gather you out of the nations where I sent you and bring you home again to your own land."

What a promise! Can you believe it for yourself? Can you trust that God is speaking to you? Will you take a minute and meditate on these four verses? What are they saying to you in your present situation?

Here's what they say to me:

I know you are discouraged right now, but take heart. I have a plan. You may not understand what is going on, but trust Me. My plan for you is good; it is not to destroy you. Come to Me and search for Me and you will find Me. I will answer you. I promise in the end it will all work out for your good. I want above all things an intimate relationship with you. All the things I allow in your life have purpose, and that purpose is so that I can bring you home to Me. Trust Me in this and see what I will do.

Now, I want to invite you to re-read Jeremiah 29:11-14 again. Ask God to show you what He is saying *specifically* to *you* concerning *your* particular situation. Write your thoughts:

_____
_____
_____
_____
_____
_____
_____

In the next session we will look at the promises of purpose, destiny and freedom from fear as we read Hosea 2:15.

CHAPTER 15
"Life Changing Fruit"

"Say to the righteous
That it shall be well with them,
For they shall eat the fruit of their doings."
Isaiah 3:10

The first promise we studied was the promise to receive comfort in our wilderness. I encourage you to continue listening for God's voice of comfort in the days to come. You will need to hear His voice to silence all the other voices that try to control your life. This is the foundation for everything we study. Learning to hear God's voice over all others is a lifetime journey. As we learn to ignore the other voices we become stronger and find peace in the midst of the storm.

Let's continue with Hosea 2:15 and take a look at the second and third promises God has given us. They are the promises of purpose and destiny, and of freedom from fear.

Hosea 2:15 says;

> "I will give her her vineyards from there, And the valley of Achor as a door of hope; She shall sing there, as in the days of her youth, As in the day when she came up from the land of Egypt."

Let's look at the meaning of *vineyard* so that we can understand what God is doing at this point in our journey. We know that we have been brought to this place because He wants to slow us down enough so we can hear His voice. We realize that we had to be brought here because we were starting to self-destruct and God in His mercy saved us from ourselves.

God continues to lay out His promises for us. This one we are looking at now is that we will receive vineyards in our wilderness. How is it that we can be given a vineyard in the midst of a wilderness? Did we not learn earlier that the wilderness is a dry, barren land? That it is a land without water? How then, can we expect God to give us a vineyard?

This is precisely how God shows us His mercy and power. Our God is the God of the impossible!

In Genesis 1:1-3 we read:

> "In the beginning God created the heavens and the earth. The earth was without form, and void; and darkness was on the face of the deep. And the Spirit of God was hovering over the face of the waters. Then God said, 'Let there be light; and there was light.'"

This is incredible! This is a picture of our lives! Just imagine God hovering over you right now and speaking light into your darkness. Imagine Him filling all the voids in your life. Imagine Him creating something beautiful out of your life.

In our story, the vineyard has been taken away and the promise is that God is going to return it to her. He has promised that she will sing there as she did earlier in her life. This speaks of happiness and joy. He promises she will be singing as when she came up from the land of Egypt. So, what does Egypt have to do with anything?

Egypt in the Bible represents slavery or bondage. God's people were under the oppression of Pharaoh and their lives were spent building his empire. How can we relate to that? This is my thinking. When we are serving other *gods* and chasing them, we are under the bondage of the devil. We become his slave. Everything we do benefits him and his kingdom while at the same time it is destroying us.

> **"***The promise here is that while we are in the wilderness, we will get our lives back and be set free from serving the devil!***"**

The promise here is that while we are in the wilderness, we will get our lives back and be set free from serving the devil!

Ephesians 5:8 says;

> "For you were once darkness, but now you are light in the Lord. Walk as children of light."

Here we see that as we move from the devil's kingdom into God's we are becoming something totally new.

I was reading about vineyards to get a better understanding about what we are looking at and I found something very interesting. I read that vineyards are tended during mid-June to mid-August. It is said of the grape vines that during the heat of the summer, they begin to bloom and start the slow process of developing!

Can you believe this? It is in the hottest, driest, most miserable part of the year that the vines bloom! What a discovery! When we are locked up, we are prime candidates for this very thing. God wants to see you bloom, blossom, and begin to develop right where you are! He wants to be sure that your life (your vineyard) starts producing good fruit, leaving the bad fruit behind to wither and die.

You may be wondering how God is going to do this for you. How can He take your present situation and turn it around for good? Read with me Psalm 80:14-19. The author gives us here the first step to realizing these promises:

> "Return, we beseech You, O God of hosts;
> Look down from heaven and see,
> And visit this vine.
> And the vineyard which Your right hand has planted,
> And the branch that You made strong for Yourself.
> It is burned with fire, it is cut down;
> They perish at the rebuke of Your countenance.
> Let Your hand be upon the man of Your right hand,
> Upon the son of man whom You made strong for Yourself.
> Then we will not turn back from You;
> Revive us, and we will call upon Your name.
> Restore us, O LORD God of hosts;
> Cause Your face to shine,
> And we shall be saved!"

This is our first step. We need to call upon God to come *visit us* in our wilderness, *shine His face upon us*, and *restore us* to be what we need to be. It is His doing. It is His power that enables us to be who we should be. It is His strength that carries us through. It is all about Him, not about what we can try to do on our own.

Take a minute to call out to God. Let Him know your frustrations and how you have tried to do it alone. Let Him know how you feel about where you are. Ask Him to show you what fruit He desires to cultivate in your life. Write your prayer out so that you can come back to it sometime in the future and see how far you've come.

_____

_____

_____

_____

_____

_____

_____

As we continue to seek God and what He wants to accomplish in us during our wilderness time, let's look at the different kinds of fruit we produce and where they come from.

The Bible separates fruit into two categories. One category is called the works of the flesh. The other is called the fruit of the Spirit. The works of the flesh are those things we do and the attitudes we have that are self-serving and evil. The fruit of the Spirit is the way we live as we are led by the Holy Spirit and God is in control of our lives.

Let's read about them from the Bible in Galatians 5:19-26:

> "Now the works of the flesh are evident, which are: adultery, fornication, uncleanness, lewdness, idolatry, sorcery, hatred, contentions, jealousies, outbursts of wrath, selfish ambitions, dissensions, heresies, envy, murders, drunkenness, revelries, and the like; of which I tell you beforehand, just as I also told you in time past, that those who practice such things will not inherit the kingdom of God.
>
> But the fruit of the Spirit is love, joy, peace, longsuffering, kindness, goodness, faithfulness, gentleness, self-control. Against such there is no law. And those who are Christ's have crucified the flesh with its passions and desires. If we live in the Spirit, let us also walk in the Spirit. Let us not become conceited, provoking one another, envying one another."

Re-read the portion that tells us what the works of the flesh are.

List them below. Add to this list anything you recognize in yourself that would belong in this category:

_____

_____

_____

_____

_____

Take a moment to reflect on your life. Do you remember acting out the works of the flesh? What triggered you to do so? Can you think of anything that might help keep you from acting this way?

_____

_____

_____

_____

_____

_____

Now, list the fruit of the Spirit:_____

_____

_____

_____

_____

Obviously God wants us to live our lives by walking in His Spirit and producing His fruit. He does not want us to be acting out the works of the flesh. The *works of the flesh* bring nothing but strife, death, and destruction. But the fruit of the Spirit will bring all good things. How do we change from acting out the works of the flesh to living out the fruit of the Spirit?

The Bible gives us the answer right after it lists the fruit of the Spirit. It says, *"And those who are Christ's have crucified the flesh with its passions and desires."* (Galatians 5:24)

We must act against our fleshly desires and crucify them. What does that mean? It means that we must take active control of our desires and put them to death. We must not allow them to live in our lives. We must starve them. How can we do that? We simply must not feed them.

I will give you an example. Say for instance, a friend has called and wants to meet you down the street. You know what that meeting will bring. You may end up being tempted to do something you know you shouldn't do. It may end up in a drug deal or worse.

You know from past experience being with this person always leads to something bad. What you need to do when this person calls is to crucify your desires and say no. Just say no. End of story. It is the simplest yet hardest thing to do. Saying no to wrong desires is crucifying the flesh.

The battle is in our minds. It always starts in our minds. We get a thought. We think about that thought. We analyze what we are thinking about. We weigh the pros and cons. We think about it more. Then we give in to that thought. Then we act on that thought.

Every time we do something, it has started with a thought. Whether the thing is good or bad makes no difference, it started with a thought. Do we have any control over our thoughts? Some of us may be tempted to say no, therefore shunning any responsibility. When in reality, yes, we can have control over our thoughts. As with anything else, God has a solution. He does not leave us helpless. He gives us instructions on how to deal with the thoughts in our minds.

We find this instruction in 2 Corinthians 10:3-5. We read:

> "For though we walk in the flesh, we do not war according to the flesh. For the weapons of our warfare are not carnal, but mighty in God for pulling down strongholds, casting down arguments and every high thing that exalts itself against the knowledge of God, bringing every thought into captivity into the obedience of Christ."

"When we have a thought, one that we know is contrary to what God would have for us, we must dismiss it as not valid and not entertain it."

What does this mean for us? It means that when we have a thought, one that we know is contrary to what God would have for us, we must dismiss it as not valid and not entertain it. We must decide right then and there that we will not pursue it. We must take a stand against the things that we know Jesus would not want for us. We must just say no.

Anyone who has tried to quit smoking or stay on a diet knows what we are talking about here. You get this idea in your head; *Boy a chocolate candy bar would sure taste good,* or *Just one smoke, that's all.* I won't have another one. We've all done this with many things; drugs, alcohol, personal relationships, you name it. It all starts in the mind. It is like planting a seed in the ground and watering it. The more water you put on it, the faster it will grow.

It's just like that with the things we think. If we keep watering those bad thoughts by justifying them and entertaining them, eventually they will grow into full blown actions. The Bible says we need to cast down those thoughts before they can take root and grow.

For example: You get this thought that maybe just one hit off that joint won't hurt. Or, that one swig off your buddy's bottle is just a thirst quencher. Your mind tells you, "After all, it's really hot out. It's only one swig." What about this one, "Nobody will ever know?" These are the types of thoughts that if not cast down, will grow in a short period of time and you will find yourself partaking in something you know you shouldn't.

Take some time to think about what you think!

List some thoughts that got you into trouble because you didn't dismiss them when they first came. (This would be a good exercise to do every day.)

_____

_____

_____

_____

_____

_____

_____

Now I am going to give you an opportunity to look at what you have just written and see how the outcome could have changed if you had been able to *cast down that thought.*

What if you had been able to say:

"No, I'm not going there. I will go where God sends me."
"No, I'm not doing that. I will do what God tells me to do."
"No, that's not a good place for me to be. I want to be where God is"
"No, I can't hang out there. I need to hang out with God's people."
"No, that's not something I want to put in my body, I'm God's."
"No, I'm not going to think that, it's mean, it's nasty. I am going to
 think good things."

These are the kinds of thoughts we need to use as weapons to win the battle in our minds. After we dismiss the evil thought, we need to replace it with God's thoughts. This is how we cast down arguments and bring every thought into the obedience of Christ. When it sounds like the devil, throw it out!

Write in your own words thoughts you might use to fight the battle in your mind, the battle you are struggling with now.

_____

_____

_____

_____

_____

_____
_____

_____

If you can win the battle in your mind, you will win the battle with your flesh. If you win the war over your flesh, you will walk in the Spirit. You *will no longer be prisoner* of your flesh, but *you will walk in freedom* through the power of God's Holy Spirit.

Instead of being angry, manipulative, and living in all manner of evil, you will be walking in the fruit of the Spirit which is love, joy, peace, longsuffering, kindness, goodness, faithfulness, gentleness, and self-control.

This is the fruit He wants to bloom, blossom, and begin to develop in you while you are locked up and in the wilderness.

> Finally brethren,
> Whatever things *are* true
> Whatever things *are* noble,
> Whatever things *are* just,
> Whatever things *are* pure,
> Whatever things *are* lovely,
> Whatever things are of good report,
> If *there is* any virtue
> And if *there is* anything praiseworthy—
> Meditate on these things.
> (Philippians 4:8)

CHAPTER 16
"Destiny's Door"

"Her uncleanness *is* in her skirts;
She did not consider her destiny;
Therefore her collapse was awesome;
She had no comforter.
"O LORD, behold my affliction,
For the enemy is exalted!"
Lamentations 1:9

During this session of our study, we will be focusing on the valley of Achor and what God is saying to us about the *door of hope*. Once again, I will write out the verse so we can refresh our memories.

Hosea 2:15:

"I will give her her vineyards from there,
And the Valley of Achor as a door of hope,
She shall sing there,
As in the days of her youth,
As in the day when she came up from the land of Egypt."

To understand this portion of our study, we need to learn what Achor is, and what it means in the Bible. The word Achor means, *trouble, disturbance, and affliction*. Would you consider being locked up a place like that? I am sure we would agree that being locked up is not a pleasant place to be; that it is a place of trouble, disturbance, and affliction.

Now that we understand what Achor means, let's continue by looking at what happened in the Valley of Achor. Then we can look at our lives with hope. We will once again see a promise of God being fulfilled as we spend time being locked up. Remember, the promise we are learning about is God's promise of *destiny and purpose.*

Our story unfolds as we read about a place called Jericho. Jericho was a city that God was going to give to a leader by the name of Joshua. They were to have victory and take over the city. There was a problem though. There was someone in their midst who did not obey God's instructions. God had instructed them not to take anything except gold, silver, bronze, and iron. Those things were to be used as an offering to Him.

There was a man by the name of Achan who took a Babylonian garment, some silver, and some gold and buried them by his tent. This was in direct opposition to the instructions God had given them. Joshua found out his secret and approached him. Achan says in the Bible,

> "...Indeed, I have sinned against the Lord God of Israel, and this is what I have done: When I saw among the spoils a beautiful Babylonian garment, two hundred shekels of silver, and a wedge of gold weighing fifty shekels, I coveted them and took them. And there they are, hidden in the earth in the midst of my tent, with the silver under it." (Joshua 7:20-21)

This was his downfall. He coveted something that was forbidden. He went after the lust of the flesh rather than being led by God's Spirit. *And then he tried to hide what he did.*

I am sure what happened to Achan is what we just finished discussing in the last chapter. He knew what they were permitted to take but he saw something he wanted that was not on God's list. He might have thought, *I'd like to have that. What harm will it do to take it? Nobody has to find out. I'll just bury it while no one is looking.*

The problem with his thinking was that although no one else saw him, *God did.* When Achan confessed his wrongdoing, Joshua sent messengers to uncover his booty. Achan's fate was sealed. All the things he buried, all his animals, his family, and all his possessions were taken with him to the Valley of Achor. Instead of living in community in victory, Achan and his family perished in the Valley of Achor. This story helps us understand the meaning of Achor as *trouble.*

God sees all. We've got to get this in our heads. God sees everything. He saw what Achan did. We cannot hide from God. We can deceive others and even ourselves, *but we cannot deceive God.*

"*We cannot hide from God. We can deceive others and even ourselves, but we cannot deceive God.* "

The sad part about this is that Achan is not the only one who suffered. His whole family suffered the same fate. We must realize that the choices that we make do not only affect us, but those around us as well. I would encourage you to read the whole story; you can find it in Joshua chapters six and seven. The key verses are Joshua 6:18-19 and Joshua 7:19-21.

Let's read from the Bible about our *hidden stuff*; that dirty laundry we think we have hidden in a basket in the back of a dark closet with the door bolted shut.

Matthew 10:26 says;

> "Therefore do not fear them. For there is nothing covered that will not be revealed, and hidden that will not be known."

These are Jesus' words, written in red in my Bible. We can be sure the stuff we try to hide one day will be seen.

1Corinthians 3:13 tells us;

> "Each one's work will become clear; for the Day will declare it, because it will be revealed by fire; and the fire will test each one's work, of what sort it is."

Those two verses are enough to *make me think*. What is in your closet that you have buried thinking no one will ever find? This question is one I will not ask you to write about but encourage you to get in *your prayer closet with God* and find out how He wants you to set things right.

Eventually our dirty laundry lands us in the Valley of Achor. It catches up with us and we pay. Don't let any of it keep you from the promises that are yours. Don't live one more minute carrying the weight of that stuff. You can come clean with God. Guess what? He already knows everything just like He knew what Achan did. He's giving you a way out right now. Take the time and get serious. Pull that laundry basket out of the closet and face it today. Give it to Him one piece at a time. *Let Him nail it to the cross and have Jesus' blood cover it for all time.* This is your chance, don't miss it. Take some time before you continue reading to make peace with God.

Pause - Reflect - Meditate

Have we committed sin against God like Achan? We all have. Have we brought things into our lives that we know God forbids? Are we in the Valley of Achor (trouble) now because of what we have done?

> **"The choice is yours. You can look at your present situation as hopeless because you feel hopeless or you can look at it as an opportunity to find God."**

If the answer is yes, *there is still hope.* How can I say that? Because God says so in Hosea 2:15. How does this relate to you? *He is giving you the Valley of Achor as your gateway to hope.*

The choice is yours. You can look at your present situation as hopeless because you feel hopeless or you can look at it as an opportunity to find God. You can take the *trouble* you find yourself in and look for God in the middle of it. You can cry out to Him to show you this door of hope. Even in your sorrow, you can reach out to Him with a mustard seed of faith. I promise you He will be there.

You may be thinking, *how am I supposed to believe that this trouble can bring me hope?* I am going to present to you Someone who is your door to hope.

This door is a Person. *This door is Jesus.* Remember earlier that we read that Christ is our hope? (I Timothy 1:1) Let's look at some more verses from the Bible to help us understand.

John 10:7-9, Jesus is speaking here. He says,

> "Most assuredly, I say to you, I am the door of the sheep. All who ever came before Me are thieves and robbers, but the sheep did not hear them. I am the door. If anyone enters by Me, he will be saved, and will go in and out and find pasture."

Here is our door of hope! Here is the door that will lead us out of the Valley of Achor. Here is the One who wants to step into our wilderness and lead us out. It is Jesus! He is the One who wants to carry us through our trouble and *give us hope.*

It is in the Valley of Achor, *our valley of trouble* where we will encounter the great open door! He will lead us and guide us. He will walk with us through our valley and give us hope. He will show us the door, He will give us Himself.

The remaining part of Hosea 2:15 says:

> "...She shall sing there,
> As in the days of her youth,
> As in the day when she came up from the land of Egypt."

This part of the verse tells us that we will sing in the valley. How can that be? It can only be when we recognize that *Jesus is our hope*. When He is standing in the midst of our trouble, we have the opportunity to receive comfort and peace. He is the One who stilled the waters in the storm. *He is the One who crawls into jail or prison with us and is not afraid to stand by us.* He is the One who speaks in the dark night when all the lights are out and our tears fall.

He is the One who holds you when you are shaking with fear. He is the One who brings you courage when all you can do is wait. He is the door to hope! He is your *door to hope*. Won't you make your way toward that open door? Won't you let your heart trust just a little bit? I promise, before you take that first step, He is already coming toward you. His arms are wide open to receive you.

When is the last time you have been hugged? When is the last time someone cared about you without wanting something from you? Come to Jesus, your door to hope. Your heart will sing if you will let Him in and love you like only He can.

You will find peace and hope leaning on the chest of Jesus. You will hear His heartbeat of love for you. He will not harm you, use you, or discard you. He will receive you and keep you. You need not do anything but come as you are.

As you spend time with Jesus, He will show you purpose and destiny for your life. He will breathe in His breath of life and revive you. Stay in His presence as long as you can. *Feel His embrace of perfect love.* Hope has embraced you. It's time you embraced the Person of hope.

Pause - Reflect - Meditate

HELP! I'm Locked Up and I Need... HOPE!

Use the following lines to journal your thoughts and reflections:

_____

_____

_____

_____

_____

_____

_____

_____

_____

_____

_____

_____

_____

_____

_____

_____

_____

_____

_____

_____

CHAPTER 17
"Changing Clothes"

"Let us be glad and rejoice and give Him glory,
for the marriage of the Lamb has come, and
His wife has made herself ready.
And to her it was granted to be
Arrayed in fine linen, clean and bright, for
the fine linen is the righteous acts of the saints.
Then he said to me, "Write: Blessed are
those who are called to the marriage
supper of the Lamb!"
Revelation 19:7-9

We are now ready to move on to the fourth promise of God. We will be reading from the Life Recovery Bible:

Hosea 2:16:   "When that day comes," says the Lord.
you will call me 'my husband,'
instead of 'my master.'"

Hosea 2:19-20:   "I will make you my wife forever,
showing you righteousness and justice,
unfailing love and compassion.
I will be faithful to you and make you mine,
and you will finally know me as the LORD."

The fourth promise is that *we will no longer be slaves, but brides*. How awesome is that? We will no longer look at God as a harsh taskmaster who we can never please, but as One who

---

loves us unconditionally; One who shows us kindness, tenderness, and is faithful to us for all time. How can we fathom such a loving God? He says we will be His forever, that He will be bound to us by His love and mercy!

Write the fourth promise on the line below. Receive it as you write:

I will no longer be a slave, but a bride:

_____

Hosea 2:16 begins by saying, *"And it shall be in that day."* What day?

The day of our wilderness, our Valley of Achor, our time of trouble. That is the day! This is the day! Right now! During the time we are locked up, we are promised that we will know God in a new and special way. We will know the side of Him we have never experienced before. We will see His tenderness, His kindness, and it will cast out all our fear.

1John 4:18 says that perfect love casts out fear. Let's read it:

> "There is no fear in love; but perfect love casts out fear, because fear involves torment. But he who fears has not been made perfect in love."

The Life Recovery Bible says it this way:

> "Such love has no fear, because perfect love expels all fear. If we are afraid, it is for fear of punishment, and this shows that we have not fully experienced his perfect love."

Who but God could love us perfectly?

In 2Timothy 1:7 we read:

> "For God has not given us a spirit of fear, but of power and of love and of a sound mind."

There is no fear when we recognize God's love for us. We can walk through our days no matter what is happening without fear. If we trust that God's ways are always right and good, we don't have to fear. If we are feeling tormented with fear, we can come to God and ask Him to show us His love. Once we recognize *He is for us and not against us*, we will have peace and our fears will go away.

"This is the day the LORD has made; We will rejoice and be glad in it." (Psalm 118:24) *Today* is the day to receive this promise. *Today* is the day you can look at yourself differently. You

can tell yourself that you are worth loving, you are worth receiving mercy, and you are worth being His forever. It is up to you.

Reach out your hand right now and say;

"God, I receive this promise of Yours today. I receive by faith that I am no longer a slave to fear of what You will do to me, but I am Yours forever and You have tied Yourself to me by Your love and tender mercy. I receive by faith that all the promises of Hosea are mine simply because You love me. I receive by faith that You have brought me to this place to help me understand Your perfect love for me."

God is the perfect husband, brother, and friend. Many of us have had bad experiences with men, with husbands, or with fathers. But God is perfect. He is the perfect provider, protector, and One to rely on. He is calling you right now to His side forever. Will you answer the call and simply say, *"Here I am, I'm Yours?"*

Are you a slave or a bride? Are you afraid of God, or do you stand in awe of how much He loves you as His priceless bride and daughter? Have you ever thought you could be as close to God as this verse tells us we can?

Write out your thoughts on this:_____
_____
_____
_____
_____

Let's stop here for a minute and let me ask you a couple of questions. How do you view yourself? Are you walking with the slave mentality or the bride mentality? What does it mean to you to be a slave? What does it mean to you to be a bride?

Write your responses here and give an explanation of why you think the way you do. Don't be in a hurry with this. Use extra paper if you need to:
_____
_____
_____
_____
_____
_____
_____
_____
_____
_____

It's hard to image ourselves as a bride when we are locked up wearing issued clothing. We have become a ward of the state and our identity is hidden. We are all wearing the same clothes including our issued plastic flip flops. The last thing we feel like is a beautiful bride!

The Bible tells us in Proverbs 23:7:

> "For as he thinks in his heart, so is he..."

If we take this verse and apply it to our present situation, we see that it's very important how we think. I want to challenge you to begin to change the way you think about yourself and get your thoughts in line with what God says about you. The only way to do that is to keep reading the Bible and asking Him to show you what He wants you to know.

We have talked about many voices clamoring for our attention. This is very important as we move along in our study. God has told us here that we are destined to be His bride. At the beginning of this chapter I wrote verses out from the book of Revelation.

I want us to examine a portion of it here:

> "...the marriage of the Lamb has come and His wife has made herself ready. And to her it was granted to be arrayed in fine linen, clean and bright..." (Revelation 19:7-8)

If we look at our lives as one long courtship, an engagement so to speak, we can see the bigger picture. Everything that happens in our lives has to go through the filter of God's hands. I am not saying that He causes these things, but that He is not caught off guard by them. From the time we are born until the time we die, He is watching over us to complete what He started. His goal for every one of us is to be at the marriage supper of the Lamb.

This will be the end of history as we know it. It is the big celebration party reserved for those of us who have answered His call to become His own. It is the beginning of the new heaven and earth where all things will be wrapped up in His Son Jesus. It is the time when all tears will be wiped away and there will be no more death!

Read Revelation 21:3-4:

> "And I heard a loud voice from heaven saying, "Behold, the tabernacle of God is with men, and He will dwell with them, and they shall be His people. God Himself will be with them and be their God. And God will wipe away every tear from their eyes; there

shall be no more death, nor sorrow, nor crying. There shall be no more pain, for the former things have passed away."

Look at this and dance:

> "Then He who sat on the throne said, 'Behold, I make all things new.' And He said to me, "Write, for these words are true and faithful." (Revelation 21:5)

This is our destiny! This is what is in store for us at the end of our earthly journey! No more sorrow, no more pain, no more tears!

No more institution issued clothing! No, we will have turned in our rags for riches. Everything will be made new and perfect.

Read this and sing:

> "...To him who overcomes, I will give some of the hidden manna to eat. And I will give him a white stone, and on the stone a new name written which no one knows except him who receives it." (Revelation 2:17)

We will be given a new name, a name that is given to us by His love, a special name that we will share with him. No longer will we be, "loser," or "ugly," or "worthless." We will be known by the name He gives us!

Read this and shout:

> "Then I heard a loud voice saying in heaven, 'Now salvation, and strength, and the kingdom of our God, and the power of His Christ have come, for the accuser of our brethren, who accused them before our God day and night, has been cast down. And they overcame him by the blood of the Lamb and by the word of their testimony, and they did not love their lives to the death.'" (Revelation 12:10-11)

The lies and schemes of the devil who has tormented us our entire lives will be cast down! He will no longer have access to us because we will be forever in the bosom of God where nothing can touch us but His love!

This is our destiny my friend. All that we go through in this life is to prepare us to be His bride. Earlier we read that the bride is making herself ready. This is what life is all about, *getting ready for our wedding with King Jesus.*

Today, by faith, receive the promise that you are a bride and no longer a slave. See yourself as God does, *His special and beautiful bride.*

Trade in your issued clothing for your bridal gown!

Pause - Reflect - Meditate

Use this space to record your thoughts:

_____

_____

_____

_____

_____

_____

_____

_____

_____

_____

_____

_____

CHAPTER 18
"The Two-Sided Coin"

"I am the Vine, you are the branches.
He who abides in Me, and I in him,
bears much fruit;
for without Me you can do nothing."
John 15:5

"I can do all things through Christ
who strengthens me."
Philippians 4:13

Before we move on to the fifth promise, I want to share with you a bit of myself, my struggles, and my freedom. It is helpful for us to know someone who has come out on the other side of things. That gives us hope that we can as well.

Although I experimented with a lot of stuff, my drug of choice ended up being alcohol. Alcohol is socially acceptable, easy to acquire, and easy to write off in your mind as, *it's not so bad, I can control it*. We all know that is far from the truth. I had grown up going to church and knew I was heading in the wrong direction. I caved into the peer pressure of friends like so many of us do. The longer I ignored my conscience, the easier it was to follow these "friends" down the wrong path.

By the time I started working my first job at age eighteen, I was out of control. I believed the lie that *I could quit any time I wanted to*. The problem is that I didn't want to quit, I was having too much fun. I was *fitting in*, meeting new people, and *growing up*.

I would go to bars after work, drink until I could barely see, then get behind the wheel of my car and drive home. One night I was at a bowling alley and drank way too much. I had an orange Volkswagen at the time, a Super Beetle. Well, this particular night, the Super Beetle wasn't so super. On the way home I wrecked my car, smashing in the driver's fender. I had missed a turn on a dark, windy road. It was late at night and the road was deserted. My car died and I was scared.

> **"***I was oblivious to what was going on. In no time, sparks were flying off the fender. But I kept driving. I was on a mission. I had to get home before my mom found out.* **"**

In a panic, I turned the key and the car started. "Ok, this is good," I said. I put the car in gear and continued to drive. Because my smashed fender was resting on my front tire, it produced a lot of heat as I was driving. I was oblivious to what was going on. In no time, sparks were flying off the fender. But I kept driving. I was on a mission. I had to get home before my mom found out. Leaning forward with my nose almost touching the windshield, I labored to keep my car between the lines on the road. You know what I am talking about if you have ever driven drunk.

Because my main concern was to get home quickly, I continued to ignore the sparks coming from my car. I kept on driving until I saw flames coming from my smashed fender. I remembered that my gas tank was in the front of the car. I was still miles from home and realized even in this intoxicated state that this was not a good situation. I had sense enough to pull off to the side of the road.

I shut the car off and got out. In the corner of my eye, I saw a man coming toward me with a fire extinguisher. "Oh no!" I said. "It's a cop." I tried to straighten up as much as I could and moved away from my car. He extinguished the fire and came over to me. He told me to follow him to his car which was on the other side of the road. There was no one else on the road, no traffic, no lights, nothing.

I'm sure I smelled like a brewery but this was somewhere around 1975 and the laws weren't as strict as they are now. He wrote me a ticket, called a tow truck, and took me home. I was thankful it was late. What would my mom say if I was escorted home in a police car? I fumbled to unlock the front door and snuck into my bedroom. Finally, I passed out.

My biggest concern the next morning was what to tell my mom when she woke up and my car was gone. It was pretty simple. I told her I wrecked my car but I was OK. I told her a policeman called a tow truck for me and brought me home. I told her my car was at the body shop and I needed a ride to work. It just so happened that I worked at a Volkswagen dealer and that's where the officer had my car towed.

My mom took me to work and dropped me off. I went over to the body shop to take a look. My bright orange Super Beetle was now a two toned car. The whole front end was black. We decided mom never needed to know anything else and somehow we kept her from seeing the car. (No use in worrying her and having more explaining to do.) I can't remember how we pulled that off, but we did.

Let's think about this for a minute. I wonder how much longer I could have driven that car before the flames reached my gas tank? I wonder how long it would have taken for the car to blow up?

Do you know to this day I believe that Police Officer was an angel sent by God to be in the right place at the right time? I believe God spared my life because His plan for it hadn't even begun. I was only 18, and that was 37 years ago.

What about you? How do you view the officers or whoever picked you up and brought you to where you are? Can you view them as instruments in God's hands to spare your life, or at least to sit you down long enough so that He can talk to you?

I'm sorry to say that I didn't change my ways, nor did I realize that God spared my life that night. I continued living my way for many years, but looking back now, I know it was God who was keeping me alive.

> *"I'm sorry to say that I didn't change my ways, nor did I realize God had spared my life that night."*

I met Jesus while watching a Billy Graham crusade in my living room one day. I was too hung over to change the channel so I just let it drone on. I was in my kitchen trying to do something for the intense headache I had when Billy Graham said something that stopped me in my tracks. I sat on my couch and asked God to forgive me for running my life the way I was and asked Him to get at the steering wheel so to speak. I was all alone in the house. No music, no pleading from a preacher, just Jesus and me.

I have been clean and sober since. I have exchanged booze for the *New Wine* that the Bible speaks of. I have been delivered from my life of destruction, addiction, and selfishness, and been given a life of meaning and purpose.

I am no different than you. God does not love me any more than He loves you. Why not trust Him today to take your pain, rebellion, and addictions and give you a new life? No matter how colorful your story is, He is waiting and willing to make sense out of your life, and give you a future and a hope. (Jeremiah 29:11-14)

In the space below, write down some things you wish were out of your life. It may be addictions, people, cursing, attitudes, bad memories, anything. Just jot them down. After you do that, we will resume our study by looking at promise number five.

_____

_____

_____

_____

Write out promise number five:

I will be set free from my sin and addictions:

_____

Hosea 2:17:

> "For I will take from her mouth the names of the Baals,
> And they shall be remembered by their name no more."

If you recall, the Baals are those *other gods*" that we follow in our lives. They are the things we put in place of God. They are the attitudes, addictions, and ways of life we live that are contrary to the ways of God. We want to be delivered from them but realize we can't do it on our own. We've tried so hard and we've not succeeded. Where is our hope then?

> **"*We will be passionate about the things of God. Our lives will be completely different.* "**

What do you think it means, "I will take from her mouth the names of the Baals and they shall be remembered by their name no more?" The way I see it, the taste for those things we have been using to fulfill our lives will become bitter in our mouths. We will walk away from them and not look back. We will *no longer be slaves* to our passions or be abused by our addictions. We will be passionate about the things of God. Our lives will be completely different. Instead of hopelessness, sadness, and addiction, they will be full of hope, peace, and freedom.

At times as I am ministering in Moss Justice Center, I use stories from my life to show the power of God to deliver. I was so used to drinking that I had a hard time carrying on a conversation with someone without having a can or bottle in my hand. I was so insecure in myself that I had to hide behind the drink. I never thought I would quit drinking. It was just who I was.

I tell the ladies in the detention center that if someone would have told me years ago that I would be preaching the gospel of Jesus Christ in there, I would have told them they must be on drugs! Never in my wildest imagination would I have believed that I would be doing what I am doing.

> *"Just as I was delievered from alcohol and the many other gods I was serving, you can be delivered as well."*

Again, I am no different than you. God had a plan for my life before I was even born and that was to minister in the jail and write books. It did not matter, nor was He concerned that I chose to veer off His path for many years. He kept His eye on me and protected me until I was ready and willing to respond to Him.

Just as I was delivered from alcohol and the many other gods I was serving, you can be delivered as well. This is a promise from God. Can you believe it for yourself today? Will you take God at His word and believe you have a new life in Him waiting for you? Can you see that God loves you so much, (just like He did me) that He sent an angel to stop you from your self-destruction?

I encourage you to thank God that He sent someone into your life to extinguish the fire that was about to hit your gas tank and blow you to smithereens. Thank God that He has spared you and put you in a place where you can regroup and start over.

Will you thank Him with me today? Will you look at your present situation as God's love for you? I encourage you to write about an event in your life that may have been similar to mine. Write about a time you remember God saving your life when you were acting out. Then thank Him for it. Who are the angels He sent and how did He send them? Thank God for them and pray a blessing over their lives._____

_____

_____

_____

_____

_____

_____

_____

Next, I would like to examine the verses that are written at the beginning of this chapter. They are two sides of a coin. This is a million dollar coin that we need to be able to withdraw from our memory's bank at a moment's notice.

I am going to ask you to write them out and memorize them. They will change the way you look at things and change your life.

John 15:5
"...without Me you can do nothing."

_____

Philippians 4:13
"I can do all things through Christ Who strengthens me."

_____

As we return to our fifth promise in Hosea, we see that God is saying here, "I will take from her mouth the Baals." It is God who is taking the action so that our lives can be changed. We have tried all sorts of solutions that have not worked. We have spent time in jail, prison, rehab, recovery groups, the hospital, and maybe even tried medication to overcome our hang ups and addictions. These attempts are not bad, but if we rely on them and our ability to make them work, we will fail every time. The Bible is very clear when it tells us we can do nothing without God. It is also very clear that with God we can do anything. God's promise *to us is that He will do it for us* while we are in the wilderness. While we are locked up, we can *expect God to help us* change the way we live as we recognize our inability to do it on our own.

This is the coin I want to give you. On one side we realize we can't do it, but on the other we realize we can. The defining factor is God. If God is in the equation, all things are possible!

Every time I leave Moss Justice Center, I am amazed at what my life has turned out to be. That loud mouth drunk has become a trumpet for the delivering power of Jesus Christ.

What about you? Can you see yourself differently? Do you believe *there's got to be more to your life than just surviving one more day?* Do you believe God wants to take your life and change it so dramatically that you will have a hard time believing what it has turned out to be?

I challenge you to see beyond what you see, to hear beyond what you hear in the natural. See what God sees. Hear what God says.

_____

This is the two sided coin:

Without Him you can't do anything,
But with Him you can do everything.

CHAPTER 19
"Calm the Chaos"

"Then He arose and rebuked the wind,
and said to the sea,
"Peace, be still!"
And the wind ceased
and there was a great calm."
Mark 4:39

We are now ready to examine the sixth promise of God in Hosea 2:18.

Let's read it from the Life Recovery Bible:

> "On that day I will make a covenant with all the wild animals and the birds of the sky and the animals that scurry along the ground so they will not harm you. I will remove all weapons of war from the land, all sword and bows, so you can live unafraid in peace and safety."

Do you remember at the beginning of this study what we said about the wilderness? We said that it can be a dangerous place because wild animals and hostile tribesmen roam around. It's a place where you have to watch your back every minute. You can never let your guard down. You must always be alert and ready to defend yourself.

As we have moved through this study, we have tried to be as honest as we can with ourselves and God. We have examined our lives and seen them in the light of Hosea's story. We have come to realize there is a reason for our wilderness; that there is a purpose for us being locked up. We have been encouraged to see God's promises for us and receive them as our own.

The sixth promise we are going to look at is the promise that in the midst of all our craziness, God has made provision for us to live unafraid in peace and safety. That's what Hosea 2:18 tells us. Can you imagine living in peace and safety while being locked up?

"I just want peace!" How many times have you heard that or perhaps said it yourself? "Give me some peace!" With many voices shouting at us from inside and out, we hold our heads in our hands and want to scream "Stop, I can't take it anymore!" We can't sleep. We can't eat. We toss and turn in our beds until we get up. We rise to another day of exhaustion, stress, and anxiety.

> **"*Just as we tend to look for love in all the wrong places, we tend to do the same with peace. We try to drown our sorrows and failed expectations in a bottle, pills, men, or women.*"**

We are irritable and short tempered. We might get into a fight and find ourselves locked down. Now we are isolated, written up, and losing good time. That just adds to our depression, frustration, and anger. Unfortunately, this cycle repeats itself more times than we would like to admit. What is the answer? Where can we find relief?

Just as we look for love in all the wrong places, we tend to do the same with peace. We try to drown our sorrows and failed expectations in a bottle, pills, men, or women. We look for peace by running away from our responsibilities thinking that less to worry about will help.

Just what is peace? If you remember, when we were studying hope, we found that *hope is a Person*. And that Person is Jesus Christ.

We looked at 1 Timothy 1:1 and it said:

> "Paul, an apostle of Jesus Christ, by the commandment of God our Savior and the Lord Jesus Christ, our hope.

The same goes for peace. *Peace is a Person*. And that Person is Jesus Christ.

In Ephesians 2:13 -14 we read:

> "But now in Christ Jesus you who once were far off have been brought near by the blood of Christ. For He Himself is our peace..."

This is pretty clear. We were far from God. We had no peace. Jesus' blood allows us access to God. *Jesus is our peace.* We are able to come to God because of what Jesus has done for us. I want to share with you two life changing verses in the Bible. They have changed the way I view the struggles I deal with. I hope they will do the same for you. They both are talking about Jesus.

Hebrews 4:15-16:

> "For we do not have a High Priest who cannot sympathize with our weaknesses, but was in all points tempted as we are, yet without sin. Let us therefore come boldly to the throne of grace, that we may obtain mercy and find grace to help in time of need."

Hebrews 2:17-18:

> "Therefore, in all things He had to be made like His brethren, that He might be a merciful and faithful High Priest in things pertaining to God, to make propitiation for the sins of the people. For in that He Himself has suffered, being tempted, He is able to aid those who are tempted."

Glory! Glory! And more glory! We are not alone in our struggles!

Do you realize what these two verses are saying to us? Have you ever heard the cliché, *Been there, done that, got the t-shirt?* This is how I interpret these verses: Jesus came to earth and walked among us. He was tempted and tested just like we are but He did not sin. He knows what we are going through!

In John 1:14 we read:

> "And the Word became flesh and dwelt among us, and we beheld His glory, the glory as of the only begotten of the Father, full of grace and truth."

Jesus walked among the people. He was fully man, yet fully God. When He came to earth, He walked as a man in total connection to God. He experienced the same hurts and temptations that we do and understands where we are coming from.

His friends deserted Him when He needed them the most. They fell asleep in the garden while He was in agony and sweating blood. They scattered when the authorities took Him to trial. Does this sound familiar? If it does, Jesus knows how you feel. You've got Him on your side. *You are not alone.*

Isaiah 53:3-8 paints a picture of Jesus for us. It reminds us of how He suffered the same pain and rejection that we do. It reminds us of how He can relate to every situation we find ourselves in.

Read with me from the Life Recovery Bible:

> "He was despised and rejected--a man of sorrows, acquainted with deepest grief. We turned our backs on him and looked the other way. He was despised, and we did not care. Yet it was our weaknesses he carried; it was our sorrows that weighed him down. And we thought his troubles were a punishment from God, a punishment for his own sins! But he was pierced for our rebellion, crushed for our sins. He was beaten so we could be whole. He was whipped so we could be healed. All of us, like sheep, have strayed away. We have left God's paths to follow our own. Yet the LORD laid on him the sins of us all. He was oppressed and treated harshly, yet he never said a word. He was led like a lamb to the slaughter. And as a sheep is silent before the shearers, he did not open his mouth. Unjustly condemned, he was led away. No one cared that he died without descendants, that his life was cut short in midstream..."

Take some time to re-read those verses. Meditate on what Jesus did for you. Take a good look at your life and see how He paid the price for you to be set free. He did it all. He did it for you. Will you believe it today?

"Don't ever think that nobody understands or cares about what you are going through. Jesus does."

To me, the most powerful and tender verse in the Bible simply says, "Jesus wept." Look it up. You can find it in John 11:35. "Jesus wept." This was at the tomb of His good friend Lazarus. The people that watched said, "...See how He loved him!" (John 11:36) Jesus knows what it is like to have His heart broken. He knows how we suffer when we lose someone. He will come and comfort you when you need Him. Don't ever think that nobody understands or cares about what you are going through. Jesus does.

The Bible tells us that Jesus has gone through everything we do, has been tempted and tested in all ways we are, but He never sinned. This leads us to the conclusion that there is nothing in our lives that He is not familiar with. He knows what it is like to be tempted and He knows the way out.

Since Jesus knows the way out, He can show us the way. When we are tempted, we can go to

Him and expect help to overcome. When we are hurting and our hearts are broken, we can go to Him, knowing He weeps with us. There is no friend like Jesus. There is no one else we can count on to understand completely what we are going through.

Will you look to Him right now with all your pain and sorrow? Will you look to Him with all your temptation, discouragement, and strife? He is waiting with open arms inviting you to be embraced and comforted. Will you take the step toward Him today? Will you let Him be your peace right now?

It may help if you write out those things that are bothering you, tempting you, and making you miserable. After you write them out, talk to Jesus about them. Ask Him to help you.

_____
_____
_____
_____
_____
_____
_____
_____
_____
_____
_____

He is waiting and willing to be your peace. He is waiting and willing to embrace you so you will feel safe. He is waiting and willing to calm the chaos in your life.

Listen as He says to you, Peace, be still, you are safe with Me.

CHAPTER 20
"Drowning the Devil"

"that He might sanctify and cleanse her
with the washing of water by the word."
Ephesians 5:26

"above all, taking the shield of faith
with which you will be able
to quench all the fiery darts
of the wicked one."
Ephesians 6:16

Let's return now to our verse that contains the sixth promise. Read with me from The Life Recovery Bible:

Hosea 2:18:

"On that day I will make a covenant with all the wild animals and the birds of the sky and the animals that scurry along the ground so they will not harm you. I will remove all weapons of war from the land, all swords and bows, so you can live unafraid in peace and safety."

Again we read, "On that day." What day? The day we recognize that the wilderness we are in is God's way of showing us His love. It's the day we realize there is a plan and a purpose for our lives and being locked up is part of that plan. It's the day we trust God with our lives completely.

We are reminded of His care in Jeremiah 29:11:

> "For I know the thoughts that I think toward you, says the LORD, thoughts of peace and not of evil, to give you a future and a hope."

If we hear His voice, read His word, and believe what it says, we can live in freedom while being locked up. You might ask, "How can I be free when I am locked up?" Good question.

I have mentioned before during this study that I volunteer in our local County Detention Center. I can tell you what I have just written is the truth. I have seen ladies set free from all sorts of *wild animals* and *weapons of war* as they come to Jesus and let Him into their situations.

On the other hand, I also know ladies on the outside who struggle daily with things, including addictions. I have watched them go from one treatment center to another, and some never find their way out of the cycle. As a Chaplain, I spoke at the funerals of two friends who never made it out. They were not locked up in a physical jail or prison, but were in chains nonetheless.

> **"This freedom I am talking about is freedom of the heart. It is freedom that once experienced, it cannot be taken away."**

This freedom I am talking about is freedom of the heart. It is freedom that once experienced, *it cannot be taken away*. It is the freedom of knowing, not in your head, but in your heart that you are totally, unconditionally forgiven and loved. It is freedom from carrying your heavy baggage around and leaving it at the feet of Jesus. It is the relief we feel when we see Him pick up those bags, nail them to His cross, and watch them disappear. It is the freedom of victory over addictions, negative emotions, tormenting thoughts, and guilt.

Are you familiar with the movie, *The Wizard of Oz*? As a child, watching this movie was a family tradition during Christmas. One of my favorite scenes in the movie was when they killed the wicked witch of the west. She was mean. She stalked Dorothy and her friends. She antagonized them, frightened them, even tried to kill one of them by setting him on fire. She sent her flying creatures to scare them while they walked through the woods. She harassed them the whole time they were trying to get to the Wizard. They knew if they got to the Wizard, he could help them change their lives. The wicked witch did everything she could to *keep them from their destiny*.

Finally, they caught the witch and poured water over her. When she saw them coming with the water, she shrieked. She knew she was done for. She moaned and groaned throwing her arms up in the air trying to shield herself from certain death. She knew the water would destroy her. She cried out, "I'm melting, I'm melting." Everyone watched with joy as she melted in front of their eyes and all that was left of her was her drenched clothes and her black pointed hat lying in a pile on the floor. *She was no longer a threat and they were free from her forever.*

Just as the wicked witch in the movie was destroyed by water, so the devil will be destroyed as we pour water over him. What is this water? *It is the living water of Jesus. It is the Word of God. It is what's in the Bible.* As we study, learn, and make the Word of God a daily reality, the devil is destroyed. We can take the Word of God like the people in the Wizard of Oz did and pour it over the works of the devil in our lives, and he will be snuffed out; just like the wicked witch of the west was.

David describes Jesus in Psalm 22:14:

> "I am poured out like water..."

In John 19:34 we read:

> "But one of the soldiers pierced His side with a spear, and immediately blood and water came out."

On the cross, Jesus poured out His life like water. On the cross, His side was punctured causing blood and water to flow. It was at Calvary that Jesus' life was poured out so we can be free.

It is the living water of Jesus' life, death, and resurrection that gives us hope and victory over the devil. It is this water that we have as our weapon against all his conniving schemes. His schemes are no match for the power of Jesus' cross. His weapons are inferior. No matter what the devil throws at us, we can win. *We can be every bit as free from him as the people in the Wizard of Oz were from the wicked witch of the west.*

> **"It is the living water of Jesus' life, death, and resurrection that gives us hope and victory over the devil."**

Do you believe it? Can you imagine living with freedom of the heart? Can you imagine, even while locked up, feeling totally, unconditionally loved and accepted? *This freedom is yours, my dear friend.*

This kind of peace is yours. Jesus, the Prince of Peace has bought it for you. You *have been delivered* from the devil's power over you and transferred from the kingdom of darkness into the kingdom of light. (Colossians 1:13) It has already been done on the cross. *It's a done deal.*

In other words, you have been rescued from death and given new life. You have the power of the life of Jesus in you. You are free. You can walk in peace. You can hope against hope and win the battle. You have a new address. You live on the road to life now. When mail is sent to your old address, it is sent back stamped, *Addressee Unknown!*

The Life Recovery Bible says in Colossians 2:13-15:

> "You were dead because of your sins and because your sinful nature was not yet cut away. Then God made you alive with Christ, for He forgave all our sins. He cancelled the record of the charges against us and took it away by nailing it to the cross. In this way, He disarmed the spiritual rulers and authorities. He shamed them publicly by His victory over them on the cross."

Is that not TOO AWESOME? He cancelled the record of the charges against us and took it away by nailing it to the cross! We are forgiven! Our baggage has been nailed to the cross and all those things that have been controlling us all our lives have been shamed by His victory. The price was paid over two thousand years ago before we were ever born. What incredible love, what incredible relief! We no longer have to carry these heavy burdens. How can we own this promise? *Simply by believing and receiving.*

Let's pause here for a moment and thank Jesus for what He has done:

Thank You Jesus for going the distance for me. Thank You that when You carried Your cross all my sins and burdens were on Your back. Thank You that when they nailed You to the cross, all my sin and all my burdens were nailed to it with You. Thank You that when they laid You in the tomb, it was all buried with You. Thank You that when You rose from the grave, You left it all there so I can be free.

Thank You that my sins and burdens will no longer have a hold of me and rule my life. I want You to be the ruler of my life. I want to trade all my burdens for Your peace. I believe You are the Prince of Peace and if I look to You for peace, I will receive it. I look to You right now, Jesus, as my source of peace.

Thank You that the water of Your Word is my weapon against the devil. Thank You Jesus, that when I hear the devil come knocking, I will answer with a bucket of Your living water. Thank

You, Jesus that I will watch him melt into nothing as I trust in You and keep my thoughts on You. Thank You for hearing my prayer. Amen.

Write your thoughts out on *freedom from the devil* and what that means to you.

_____
_____
_____
_____
_____
_____
_____
_____
_____
_____
_____

"And you shall know the truth,
And the truth shall make you free."
John 8:32

"Therefore, if the Son makes you free,
You shall be free indeed."
John 8:36

CHAPTER 21
"Dawn of a New Day"

"But for you who fear my name,
the Sun of Righteousness will rise
with healing in His wings.
and you will go free, leaping with joy
like calves let out to pasture.
On that day when I act,
you will tread upon the wicked
as if they were dust under your feet,"
says the LORD of Heaven's armies."
Malachi 4:2-3
(Life Recovery Bible)

As we begin this chapter, I want to paint a picture for you of what I see when I read the above verses. I envision Jesus rising up from the horizon as I sit on a bench at the beach looking out over the ocean. His arms are outstretched, ready to receive me. He opens His mouth and a warm breeze gently touches my ear. Through it, He whispers, "*Come.*"

His eyes sparkle. There is so much light coming from them that their reflection dances on the water like stars that have come to life. They are kind and full of peace. They calm my soul. My heart skips, leaping with joy as I gaze into them. I am drawn to Him and feel certain I could walk on water to get to Him. *His love is that powerful.*

I rise. With every move I make toward Him, He makes two toward me. I feel the cool sand beneath my feet. I am getting closer to the water. I fix my eyes on His and keep them there. It is His love that enables me to stay focused. I feel cool water under my feet. I keep walking, He keeps walking. I smile. His love is causing me to do the impossible. I feel no fear. I will

---

not sink. His love will keep me afloat until we embrace. It is His love that heals, delivers, and enables me to walk on water. It is His love that enables me to tread on every shark, and evil thing that would try to rise up and devour me. It is His love that rises from the horizon with healing in its wings and brings me safely to Him.

I love the beach. I love everything about the beach. I remember going there with some friends during a very rough time in my life. I would sit there watching the waves coming in and going out, endlessly moving with their soothing symphony of sound. As I am typing, I can hear them now. And in the distance I hear sea gulls coming toward me ready to swoop in glorious flight. I smile inward, as I remember ducking so I would miss their "droppings."

There is something mysterious yet beautiful about the sounds at the beach. You can sit for hours not having to speak to anyone. You can get lost in your thoughts, distance yourself from your problems, and become captivated by the vastness of the sea. Or, you can simply sit and watch people interacting with each other. Children running up and down the beach, falling down with laughter, or splashing in the water is a picture of freedom to me. The carefree, whimsical motions of children bid me come and play.

> **"*I love the feel of the cool sand squishing through my toes and the crisp breeze blowing through my hair.*"**

I especially enjoy walking the beach early in the morning before the rest of the world wakes up. The earlier, the better. I love the feel of the cool sand squishing through my toes and the crisp breeze blowing through my hair. If I can get out there while the moon is still out, there is an extra special treasure waiting for me as I watch its reflection dance on the water.

As beautiful as a moonlit evening is, I anxiously await the dawn of the morning. Anticipating the glorious array of colors that pierce through the darkness, I look for a bench to sit on. Patiently waiting, I position my camera so that in a moment's time, I might be able to snap the *perfect sunrise* picture.

For me, the sunrise represents moving on. It brings with it hope and anticipation of a new day. Along with that anticipation comes gratefulness for what I have learned yesterday. Recently I wrote a poem that seems to fit in right here. I would like to share it with you:

"My Cloak"

My cloak is the sum
Of my days
Woven moment by moment,

Choice by choice.

Its color the sum of good and bad,
Light and dark,
Painted by the hand of decision.

May the sacrifice of my Redeemer,
The beautiful crimson flow,
Devour all its darkness.

May all who witness the change
Rejoice with me
At its power to transform.

As we come close to the end of our journey together, I would like to encourage you to anticipate your own *dawn of a new day*. We have learned much in our time together.

We have learned that God loves us with an everlasting love, that He is not mad at us, and that He is with us every step of the way. We have learned that the devil comes to steal, kill, and destroy, but that Jesus has come to give us a new life.

We realize that we have made some very bad decisions, but that God has a plan for our lives, and that plan is to give us a future and a hope. We have come to realize that Jesus is our hope, our peace, and our life.

As we have been studying the first two chapters in the book of Hosea, we find that we are in a wilderness and that it can be a very good thing if we recognize what is really going on. We find that God will meet us right where we are.

We have learned how to defeat the devil and have done some exercises to expose his work in our lives. We are beginning to trust God with our lives and recognize that *He is for us and not against us*.

I invite you now to read the verses at the beginning of this chapter and describe what your *dawn of a new day* looks like.

_____

_____

_____

_____

_____

_____

Before we move on to the seventh promise, we are going to take a look at some things in the Bible that will help us understand what Jesus has done for us. We will learn that as we have moved from the kingdom of darkness into the kingdom of light, we are now on the winning side. Jesus is the Ultimate winner of all time and as we put our trust in Him and His finished work on the cross, we will experience the winning side of life!

CHAPTER 22
"It is Finished!"

"So when Jesus had received the sour wine,
He said, "It is finished!"
And bowing His head, He gave up His spirit."
John 19:30

"I have glorified You on the earth.
I have finished the work
which You have given Me to do."
John 17:4

"When's it going to be over? When am I going to wake up from this nightmare?" Anyone who is in a crisis situation will ask themselves these and many other questions. At times we cannot see any light or feel anything but misery. We want to crawl into a corner shielding ourselves from any more pain. If it gets bad enough, we may cease to look for comfort or hope, ending up surviving day to day but not really living.

It is when we find ourselves in this state of mind we must go to God for hope. We need to remember what He told us when things weren't quite so bad. We need to go back to the Bible and read what He says about us. As we read His truth, the lies of the devil are cast down and *we begin to hope again*. We start to see a flicker of light and our pain begins to subside.

Earlier in our journey we discussed the fact that Jesus promised to bring to our remembrance everything that He has taught us. It is very important to keep reading the Bible so that we know who we are to God and what He says about us. With that understanding, we can battle the devil when he comes at us with his accusing voice. His demeaning threats can be cast out as we remember God's words to us. He can no longer rule us with accusing names like *loser, idiot, ugly, waste,* or any of the other things he may call us. He no longer has the authority to convince us that nothing will ever change.

Remember Jeremiah 29:11-14? This is a great place to go when you are feeling down and discouraged. Let's read this truth again. This is one passage you can never read too many times. It is a life-saver that will bring a flicker of light when all you are experiencing is darkness.

Jeremiah 29:11-14 from the Life Recovery Bible says:

> "For I know the plans I have for you," says the LORD. "They are plans for good and not for disaster, to give you a future and a hope. In those days when you pray, I will listen. If you look for me wholeheartedly, you will find me. I will be found by you," says the Lord. "I will end your captivity and restore your fortunes. I will gather you out of the nations where I sent you and will bring you home again to your own land."

I want to share something else with you that will set your sights on more than surviving another day. The truth is designed to set us free. The more truth we know, the more freedom we experience.

Let's read Isaiah 61:1 again:

> "The Spirit of the Lord GOD is upon Me
> Because the Lord has anointed Me
> To preach good tidings to the poor;
> He has sent Me to heal the brokenhearted,
> To proclaim liberty to the captives,
> And the opening of the prison to those who are bound."

This is a beautiful description of Jesus and what God wanted to accomplish with His life while He was here on earth. God sent Him here to walk among us and to show us what God is like. He was sent to heal our broken hearts and set us free from the things that chain us up. He came to be our way out of darkness.

Take these words, read them, memorize them, and digest them, so they become part of who you are. When you hear the name *Jesus* you will be reminded of what He came to do for you.

When the devil comes knocking at your heart's door, you can throw this water on him and silence him. When he reminds you of all your past mistakes and bad decisions, tell him that Jesus came to set you free from all of his accusations. Tell him that Jesus lives in you and is the ruler of your heart and that all his chatter is in vain. Let him know that you are one of Jesus' sheep and you will only listen to Jesus' voice.

When Jesus knew that His time was short, He got with His friends and attempted to explain to them what He was getting ready to go through. I want to encourage you to read John chapters 13-20. This will give you an understanding of the last moments of Jesus' life. It has been said that when people know they are dying, their last words will reveal what's most important to them. We can assume that same thing in Jesus' case. Reading these chapters with this in mind will help us realize what was most important to Him.

Pause - Reflect - Meditate

Moving along, in John 13:1 we read:

> "Now before the Feast of the Passover, when Jesus knew that His hour had come that He should depart from this world to the Father, having loved His own who were in the world, He loved them to the end."

We can expect everything that happens from this point until He dies on the cross to be the most important to Him. Everything He says and does is a revelation of His deepest thoughts and desires. As we read the words of Jesus, we get a glimpse into God's heart and find out how much we are truly loved. Jesus is our example of God. Jesus came to show us who God is and what He is like.

Read with me what Jesus says about this in John 14:8-9:

> "Phillip said to Him, "Lord, show us the Father, and it is sufficient for us." Jesus said to him, 'Have I been with you so long, and yet you have not known Me, Philip? He who has seen Me has seen the Father; so how can you say, 'Show us the Father?'"

When we see Jesus for who He is and how He feels about us, we are given the exact representation of God. Are you looking for God? Have you found Jesus? If so, you have found God.

I want to encourage you to take some time to read chapters 13-20 in John again. Ask God to show you Himself as you read about the last moments of Jesus' life; especially focus on the prayer that Jesus prayed before going to the cross. It is found in John chapter 17. It is you He is praying for in that chapter. Get some alone time and meditate on His prayer. If you do, it will change the way you think about yourself in relation to Jesus. It will remind you that He had you on His mind before He died. So many years ago, before you were ever born, you were on His mind.

Take some time to write down your thoughts on this prayer of Jesus:

_____

_____

_____

_____

_____

_____

Do you see how important you are? You were on His mind right before He died!

Let's take a look at some powerful words that He spoke right at the end. John 19:30 says, "... *It is finished!" And bowing His head, He gave up His spirit."* Matthew 27:50 records it this way, *"And Jesus cried out again with a loud voice, and yielded up His spirit."*

We clearly see that Jesus used the last bit of energy He had on the cross to shout out to the heavens that He finished what God had sent Him to do. What was He talking about?

We can find every answer we need to our questions in the Bible. What is finished?

Let's go to 1John 3:8:

> "...For this purpose the Son of God was manifested, that He might destroy the works of the devil."

That's pretty clear. Jesus came to destroy everything the devil does. Whatever the devil hits us with; Jesus has already won the victory over it. On the cross Jesus said that He destroyed the works of the devil. If that is the case, how did we end up where we are?

Although we are forgiven by God, and our record is clear in heaven, there are still consequences we have to face for our actions. For example, if we have abused our bodies with drugs and alcohol, they may begin to shut down. We get sick, hung over, or we experience more severe consequences like liver disease and other health issues. If we have sex with people we don't know, we may contract venereal diseases, hepatitis, or AIDS. If we break the law of the land, we end up in jail or prison. This is called reaping what we sow. When we sow junk, we reap junk.

That is a fact, but here is the good news. Even though there are consequences for our bad choices and decisions, our lives can be free from the junk that got us into the mess in the first place. We can move on from where we are *with hope and anticipation* of that new day that we talked about in the last chapter. We can hope against hope. Why? Because Jesus came to destroy the works of the devil and that's exactly what He did. It is not an abstract idea for someone else, *it is for you!*

Let's read about it again in Colossians 2:13-15 from the Life Recovery Bible:

> "You were dead because of your sins and because your sinful nature was not yet cut away. Then God made you alive with Christ, for he forgave all our sins. He canceled the record of the charges against us and took it away by nailing it to the cross. In this way, he disarmed the spiritual rulers and authorities. He shamed them publicly by his victory over them on the cross."

When Jesus prayed that prayer we read in John 17, He was praying for you. He was praying that you would be kept in God's hands until He comes back for you. He prayed that you would have His joy, live in His peace, and know how much you are loved. He prayed that you would be with Him always.

Take a minute to think about this. The Son of God had you on His mind, prayed for you, and asked God to keep you in His care! Out of all the prayers God receives, don't you think He is going to answer that one?

"Take a minute and think about this. The Son of God had you on His mind, prayed for you, and asked God to keep you in His care! "

Jesus shouted out on the cross, "*It is finished.*" He knew His prayer would be answered. He knew that everything He was supposed to do was completed. He has destroyed the works of the devil for all time. All we have to do is realize this and walk in it.

Let's expose the devil and his work. Let's expose him knowing that Jesus came to destroy everything that he has done and is trying to do to us right now. Let's bring the darkness out and allow the light of Jesus to swallow it up forever.

We need to be aware and watching for evidence of the devil's work against us. If you find yourself spiraling downhill quickly, do not let him win. Get some help. Talk to someone. Ask to see your Chaplain.

Light overcomes darkness. When we go into a dark room and turn the light switch on, it is no longer dark. *Darkness is swallowed up in light.* This is how it is in our lives. When we turn the light switch of Jesus on into the darkness of our lives, *the darkness has to leave.* When we expose those things that have plagued us and caused us to walk in darkness, *they lose their power over us.*

We are told in 1John 3:8 what Jesus' mission was. He came to destroy the work of the devil. In John 19:30, Jesus tells us it is finished!!!

Say it with me, "IT IS FINISHED!"

And...

"I can do all things through Christ who strengthens me
BECAUSE IT IS FINISHED."

And...

I have hope and can hope against hope
BECAUSE IT IS FINISHED."

IT IS FINISHED.

CHAPTER 23
"Full Circle"

"Then He who sat on the throne said,
"Behold, I make all things new.
And He said to me,
"Write, for these words are true and faithful."
Revelation 21:5

If we are honest with ourselves, we will admit there are times when we wonder how our lives would have turned out had we not made the decisions we made, or done some of the things we've done. As the years speed by, (it seems as though each one moves faster than the last one) I wonder where I would be right now if I had listened to my dad and gone to college. Every time I get frustrated with my job, I want to kick myself because of my rebellion. Sometimes I think that if I had gone to college my life might have turned out better. I might be making more money, be more successful, be respected, and doing something I like.

Are you like me? Do you spend time thinking about how you could have done things differently? Are there some things you said that you wish you could take back? Does your past haunt you by replaying the scenes over and over in your mind? Do you keep beating yourself up over things that you can't change?

We all do this from time to time. We've all done things we wish we didn't, and have acted in ways we know we shouldn't. But we can't change what has happened. No matter how many times we revisit the scene, the end of the movie is still the same.

Whatever caused you to land in jail or prison has happened. It cannot be changed. That is the bad news. The good news is that YOU can change. *The direction of your life can change*. You

---

can start from here and move ahead. You can let go of what was and look forward to what is to come.

Every negative can turn into a positive. Every sorrow can bring joy. Every tear can turn into hope. Every loss can cause us to grow. This is our seventh promise from God. Promise number seven tells us that we will see *new things coming from our lives*.

I'd like for you to write it out before we move on.

I will see new things coming from my life:

_____

Let's read Hosea 2:21-23:

> "It shall come to pass in that day that I will answer," says the Lord; "I will answer the heavens, and they shall answer the earth. The earth shall answer With grain, With new wine, And with oil; They shall answer Jezreel. Then I will sow her for Myself in the earth, And I will have mercy on her who had not obtained mercy; Then I will say to those who were not My people, 'You are My people!' And they shall say, 'You are my God!' "

Here we see that things have completely turned around. If you remember in Hosea 1:6, God said that He would no longer have mercy on the people. In Hosea 1:9, He says that they are not His people and He is not their God. I don't believe God had turned His back on them, but He was explaining to them what happens when they turn away from Him. In essence, He says that when we turn from Him, we cannot experience Him as our God and realize His mercy. We are too far away to reap the benefits of a good relationship with Him. But we see that something wonderful has happened between chapter one and where we are now in chapter two. *Where did things start to turn around?*

Here's what I believe to be true. When we are out there acting out and doing our own thing, God has to let us see our lives for what they are without His grace and mercy. *We have to realize that without Him, our lives are empty and meaningless.*

Until we reach out for His grace and mercy, we continue hanging out in a boat that is sinking. Our lives become unmanageable and we realize there is no life raft in the vast ocean of despair we find ourselves in. We have been allured into the wilderness. God has brought us to our knees. Our lives are not our own. We are locked up.

This is when His love shines through. Here is our seventh promise. He says in that day He will answer the heavens, and they will answer the earth. This speaks of rain. It is the end of the drought. It is the end of hot, dry summer days; the end of walking in the desert with nothing but sand in sight. It is a time of refreshing. The mirages are no longer a tease. There are pools of fresh water waiting for us to jump in. There are streams in our desert. Your parched mouth will be filled with cool water making its way to the depth of your belly. It is a promise. "I will answer," says the Lord. "I will answer."

Let's look to another passage in the Bible that talks about streams in the desert. Close your eyes a moment and picture yourself alone in the desert. It is hot and you have been traveling for days, even months or years. Your food and water have run out. You are exhausted. There is sweat pouring down your face. You taste its salt on your tongue. You look in every direction and see nothing but heat waves coming from the sand. The heat from the sand creeps up your legs. You cannot go on. You wipe the sweat off your brow with the back of your arm and collapse. Here in the heat of the day you hear a still, small voice:

Isaiah 43:18-19:

> "Do not remember the former things,
> Nor consider the things of old.
> Behold I will do a new thing.
> Now it shall spring forth;
> Shall you not know it?
> I will even make a road in the wilderness
> And rivers in the desert."

He has come to you right now and is speaking comfort and hope to your heart as you read this passage. He has plans for you, plans to give you a future and a hope. Do you remember reading that with me before? (Jeremiah 29:11-14) He will do a new thing. Are you ready?

Write Isaiah 43:18-19 out on the following lines and meditate on it.
What does it mean to you? What is God saying to you?

_____

_____

_____

_____

_____

_____

_____

_____

Let's read together Hosea 2:22:

"The earth shall answer With grain, With new wine, And with oil…"

Grain speaks of the Bread of God who is Jesus. New wine speaks of joy. Oil speaks of the Holy Spirit who is among many things, our Healer.

In John 6:48-51, Jesus explains the bread:

"I am the bread of life. Your fathers ate the manna in the wilderness, and are dead. This is the bread which comes down from heaven, that one may eat of it and not die. I am the living bread which came down from heaven. If anyone eats of this bread, he will live forever, and the bread that I shall give is My flesh, which I shall give for the life of the world."

Jesus says that as we follow Him and allow Him to feed us Himself, we will live forever. Notice, the people in the Old Testament gathered the manna and ate it every day and Jesus said they died. The manna was natural food, Jesus is spiritual food. The natural eventually dies; the spiritual lives forever.

Ephesians 5:18 in the Life Recovery Bible tells us about the new wine:

"Don't be drunk with wine, because that will ruin your life. Instead, be filled with the Holy Spirit."

Sometimes we read this passage and miss an important point. I believe there is something more to consider here than drinking and getting drunk. Obviously, getting drunk is not a good thing to do, but I see something deeper in this statement. I believe it is the issue of where we find our joy. Is our joy false due to mind altering substances, or it is genuine given to us by the Spirit of Jesus? Why would the writer compare the Holy Spirit to drink? Because everything God creates is genuine and everything the devil imitates is not.

Jesus said in John 15:11:

"These things I have spoken to you, that My joy may remain in you, and that your joy may be full."

His desire is to fill us with His joy; joy that no one can take from us. So many times I found myself alone on a bar stool in the middle of a crowd. What I am saying here is that even drinking couldn't take the loneliness away. I would drink until I couldn't see straight hoping the pain and rejection would miraculously disappear. During a night out, I would experience laughter caused by drinking, but never true joy. The next day, all I had was a whopping hang over, questions about what I had done during a black out, and the same problems I had before I started to drink. As a matter of fact, the problems seem to escalate.

The permanent solution to our problems is to know we are loved with the everlasting love that God tells us about in the Bible. (Jeremiah 31:3) When we realize we are loved that much and that God promises never to leave us, we can rest knowing that we are never alone. The need to drink or use other mind altering substances is removed as we find ourselves embraced by the love of God and tasting the new wine of His joy.

> **"*The permanent solution to our problems is to know we are loved with the everlasting love that God tells us about in the Bible. "***

Next, I would like to share with you two verses that will help us understand oil and how it symbolizes the Holy Spirit. Many of us might know the first one.

It is the 23rd Psalm:

> "The Lord is my Shepherd; I shall not want. He makes me to lie down in green pastures; He leads me beside the still waters. He restores my soul; He leads me in the paths of righteousness For His name's sake. Yea, though I walk through the valley of the shadow of death, I will fear no evil; For You are with me; Your rod and your staff, they comfort me. You prepare a table before me in the presence of my enemies; You anoint my head with oil; My cup runs over. Surely goodness and mercy shall follow me all the days of my life; And I will dwell in the house of the LORD Forever."

Here the Psalmist says that God will anoint our heads with oil and we will be comforted, free of fear, and mercy will follow us wherever we go. We will feast in the presence of our enemies and our bellies will be full of His goodness and mercy. Nothing can touch us when we recognize that we are in His tender, loving care.

We will rest beside *still waters* in the midst of our crisis knowing He's got our backs. We will be comforted and find hope in the midst of the chaos. We will *be still and know He is God*. (Psalm 46:10)

The second verse I want to share with you we have read before, but it bears repeating here.

(This is Jesus talking to the people in the synagogue.)
Luke 4:18-21:

> "The Spirit of the LORD is upon Me,
> Because He has anointed Me
> To preach the gospel to the poor;
> He has sent Me to heal the brokenhearted,
> To proclaim liberty to the captives
> And recovery of sight to the blind,
> To set at liberty those who are oppressed;
> To proclaim the acceptable year of the LORD."
>
> Then He closed the book, and gave it to the attendant and sat down. And the eyes of all who were in the synagogue were fixed on Him. And He began to say to them, "Today this Scripture is fulfilled in your hearing."

I believe Jesus was saying to the people, *You have been waiting for a redeemer, a savior, One who will come to set you free from your oppressors. I am who you have been waiting for. I have been sent by God and anointed by Him for this very thing. You don't have to wait any more. I have arrived.*

These are the promises God has given us as we walk through the wilderness with Him. He anointed Jesus for a specific mission. He anointed Him with the power of the Holy Spirit so He could accomplish that mission while He was a man on earth. His promises are as valid today as the day He read them in the synagogue.

He has come to heal our broken hearts. He has come to set us free from our oppressors. He has come to cure our blindness. He has come to tell us the good news that God's favor is upon us, *that God is for us, and He is not against us.*

We have come full circle now. We have gone from receiving no mercy to receiving mercy. We no longer feel hopeless, but hopeful.

Hosea 2:23:

> "I will sow her for Myself in the earth, And I will have mercy on her who had not obtained mercy; Then I will say to those who were not My people, 'You are My people!' And they shall say, 'You are My God.'"

AMEN AND AMEN

Epilogue

In this study I have invited you to be honest with yourself and God. We have exposed the works of the devil in your life. We have repented, prayed, and studied God's Word together. We have learned to look at our situation through the eyes of God. We have walked through the wilderness and come out on the other side as we learned of God's promises and His love. We are not where we want to be but we are not where we used to be. I believe we have made progress and the days ahead will be better for you as you apply to your life what you have learned from our study.

I would like to pray a blessing over you:

"The Lord bless you and keep you;
The Lord make His face shine upon you,
And be gracious to you;
The Lord lift up His countenance upon you,
And give you peace."
(Numbers 6:24)

This is my prayer for you as we conclude our study of Hosea and the wilderness. I trust the journey we have taken together has been of some help to you. I trust you will rely on what you have learned here when you're stuck and everything within you cries out:

"Help! I'm locked up and I need... Hope."

A special note from Ms. Lynn

It is my desire to provide copies of this workbook to ladies who are in jail or prison at no charge if they feel they would benefit from its contents.

To request a free copy of "Help! I'm Locked up...and I Need Hope!" or to get information on how to sponsor a book for someone in need, please fill out the form below and mail it to:

Lynn Potter
P.O. Box 11
York, S.C. 29710

Or email lynnpotter222@yahoo.com

Name_____

Address_____
_____
_____
_____

What are the guidelines for receiving books at the particular institution you are requesting "Help! I'm Locked up and I Need Hope!" to be sent to?
_____
_____

____   I would like to request a free book.

____   I would like more information on how to sponsor a book.
         (Please supply contact information)

         _____
         _____
         _____

Comments: Please tell me a little about yourself and your interest in this book:
_____
_____
_____

Requests for free books will be filled as sponsors become available.

Made in the USA
Charleston, SC
24 November 2011